I hope you enjoy my thoughts

God Bless

THOUGHTS BEHIND THE WORDS

A Collection of Sayings from Church Marquees and the Life Lessons They Represent.

Robert W. Ellis

DREAM
Publications
Murfreesboro, TN

www.thoughtsbehindthewords.com

Thoughts Behind the Words
A Collection of Sayings from Church Marquees and the Life
Lessons They Represent.

By Robert W. Ellis

Scriptures, unless otherwise noted, are taken from the Holy
Bible: NEW INTERNATIONAL VERSION®. Copyright ©
1973, 1978, 1984 by International Bible Society. Used by
permission of Zondervan. All rights reserved.

DREAM Publications
Murfreesboro, TN
SAN: 854-7602
Library of Congress Control Number: 2007907537

Printed in the United States of America
ISBN 978-0-9799272-0-1

CONTENTS

ABOUT THESE SAYINGS

This publication is part of a collection of sayings from church marquees obtained from our travels over several years. We keep a small notebook in the glove compartment of our car and when we encounter a saying on a church sign that appeals to us, Rhonda will make note of it. We have collected hundreds of these sayings and are still collecting. I have written my thoughts in relation to a number of these sayings, fifty-four of which I have published in this book. As space permitted, I have included other sayings, without my thoughts, which you may interpret.

ACKNOWLEDGEMENTS

I would like to thank the many people who contributed to the informational pool that collectively helped to create my thoughts.

Especially, I thank God for the influence He had on this book, so much inspiration came from Him, that He should have all the credit. I was merely the tool.

Enormous gratitude and love I express to Rhonda, my wife, best friend, and business partner for thirty-five plus years. She contributed greatly in the early stages of my adult life with good Christian behavior, supportive encouragement, entrepreneurial talents and expertise, and good food. Without her influence, well, I just don't want to think about what differences would have occurred without that influence. I love her very much.

Another special person in my life whom I want to acknowledge is my mother, whom I credit my early upbringing and devotion to what is right: from whom I received nurture and the first introduction to God and the attitude of do unto others better than you do unto yourself. I also want to acknowledge her patience while helping me as I struggled with those difficult elementary classes, such as grammar, which included my awkward spelling abilities. I love her very much.

I would like to greatly acknowledge my sister-in-law, Shirley Britt, Rhonda's sister, for her tenacious strength of endurance and for her in-depth knowledge of life, Bible, and sentence structure, which through multi-editing processes helped me present a readable manuscript, and for her encouragement. I would also like to acknowledge her husband, Bill Britt, for his encouragement, insight, example and contributing to the editing process with his two cents. I love Shirley and Bill.

The acknowledgements go on with a special thanks to John Risse, an admired advocate for Christ and the teachings of the Bible, for examining my book for flaws and doing so graciously with great remarks and insight: contributing to my strength and growth. I would like to acknowledge those special friends that for twelve months tolerated my emails and returned to me comments that were beneficial in my writing experience.

My thanks are given to *Zondervan Bible Study Library* on computer, for effortless reference supplied during my writing process. Thanks also, to Encarta® World English Dictionary [North American

Edition] © & (P) 1998-2003 Microsoft Corporation, for being there for my continual use.

As Lynn Truss said in her acknowledgements in her book *Eat, Shoots and Leaves*, "I acknowledge where faults obstinately remain, they are mine alone."

Robert W. Ellis

PREFACE

The thoughts represented here are my own, or maybe others have had the same thoughts and I have just borrowed them. Possibly the ones I borrowed them from borrowed them from someone else. It is rare to have an original thought (meaning you were the very first one to have this thought). Our entire knowledge base is derived from something others have done or said before us. It is our absorption of these actions and words that make us different. Sometimes we don't even know where our ideas are derived, but they somehow become ours. They are blended in our mind to provide us with our thoughts, our knowledge and our beliefs. From these we form what I call our constitution and in this case our spiritual constitution. I refer to our constitution as our standards to live by. These standards should not violate ethical beliefs or responsibilities, and should uphold certain traditional beliefs that do not interfere or conflict with factual truths, thereby creating our spiritual paradigm.

We should be aware of our background and try to understand where the information we base our thoughts originates. Some come from the family, some from friends, others from our readings or audio and/or video presentations, from speakers and even could include co-workers and brief acquaintances.

We are individuals and we deserve the right to develop our own personalities, lifestyles and beliefs. My question to you is, "Are we basing our life on true or false beliefs?" If new criteria are injected to our knowledge base, we should not be stubborn and ignore this, but yet analyze this new info and decide to change or stay the same.

I believe there are many talents undeveloped. By talents, I mean gifts given us by our creator. The main gift is that of a human body capable of many things and within this body is the brain. With it we can think and reason. The brain, just like a muscle, can be strengthened which can improve its capabilities and thereby improve one's existence. I believe the one thing that separates the successful from the unsuccessful is the acceptance of this fact, realizing one's potential. I also believe the major reason one does not "realize their potential" is they believe "there is no potential." This is one's "self-image." If one believes he can or believes he can't, he is correct. One can or cannot do what he believes he can or cannot do. Once one realizes this power, one can determine their future and make the choices that can change their life.

I devote my efforts to encouraging others to discover this capability within them and realize their potential. The words written in this book are written in an effort to help me discover the joys of achievement and self-gratification. My emphasis is on first consulting God with every thought and idea. I believe that every action, every word, every decision and every thought should be run by God first to get his approval or disapproval. We should simply take the information we have (The Bible and all its teachings) to establish the basis for the answer. We have a book of guidelines "an instruction manual" to help us. I believe once we run it by the "Book," we will be able to make a decision that God would approve. The "Book" provides a knowledge base that has been generated by reading and interpreting. We should also take the advice of the learned (those who have studied and are knowledgeable about the "Book") and we must blend this with our own studies to complete our spiritual constitution (paradigm).

I believe that God chose the "earth form" of Jesus so that he could announce to the world that through believing and baptism there is "hope." God is an individual God: He knows my trials, my achievements, my thoughts, my actions and is gratified when they are pleasing. I also believe that the things placed here on earth are for our enjoyment, nurture and fulfillment of life. We are offered eternal life and I believe eternal life begins here on earth. We should expect a joyous and prosperous life here on earth as well as in heaven. I present my thoughts and ideas to you for your consideration. The knowledge base that I have used comes from taking information that I have absorbed throughout my life. I am neither a preacher, theologian nor educator. I am someone who started with humble beginnings, able to live a successful life and believe I have a place in heaven. In exposing others to my beliefs, I hope to cause them to develop within themselves a strong "I can" attitude. My reason for this book is self-gratification. If the words written here give someone hope, or at the least curiosity to seek hope, then I have been gratified.

INTRODUCTION

I cannot let you read these writings with the idea that I am a perfect human being living in a perfect world. I acknowledge that I am far from such utopia. I am somewhat, OK forget the somewhat, I am a person with idealistic desires. No apologies. I believe we should strive for moral, ethical and spiritual perfection. Without these desires directing my life, I feel I would fall short of my mother's and my God's expectations, thereby falling short of my own expectations.

I am not clairvoyant, but I do believe that the future (our life) is obvious to those who believe in the power of a self-directed life. Using scripture as our guiding light, we can make the choices necessary to determine our future. I believe the past is there to direct and teach us; we learn from our mistakes and accomplishments and also from the mistakes and accomplishments of others. Today is to be lived for tomorrow and not yesterday. Tenaciously holding to yesterday's misfortunes only causes grief and worry, clogging our mind.

The writing of this book strengthened my dedication to my own self-improvement by increasing my determination to fulfill a virtuous life, pleasing to God, acknowledging my responsibilities while gaining enthusiasm to ambitiously seek knowledge with a motivation driven by God's expectations to improve all areas of my life: my earthly life and my spiritual life. This book has given me the courage to look deep within and evaluate all these things. I feel closer to God because it has enlightened areas not before realized. If you see any of yourself in my message, either positively or negatively, I hope you will pat yourself on the back if positive and talk to yourself with encouragement if negative.

I am far from perfection, but I do look to these values as a target to which I aim. Please take these directives and opinions as being omnipresent desires from God. I feel He was present during all the writings, giving me the encouragement to continue.

I would also like to acknowledge my attempt at humor. Occasionally I have tried to lighten my message with bits of humor. I feel that humor is very important in establishing and maintaining a soulful component of life: keeping us from drowning in sorrow or emotions. Laughter has been proven to extend and improve life.

I know that I have not accomplished the desired characteristics that I have preached. But, I stand firm – they are my desires.

CHOICE,
NOT CHANCE,
DETERMINES
YOUR DESTINY.

Many believe that your destiny is just how life happens, but I believe you have a choice as to how your life happens. If you believe, as so many do, you conform to your surroundings and live within a setting that is comfortable. Exposure to this comfortable setting sometimes limits us by not challenging our intelligence. I am a firm believer that one should realize their full potential and grow accordingly. If someone chooses to limit themselves, for reasons they have thought about, and prayed about, therefore coming to the conclusion that it is their desire (having made an educated choice), I have no problem with that decision. But, if you limit yourself by not realizing all things are possible, then you have, in essence, cheated yourself. God makes a place for us, but it is left to us to be the best we can be in that place. Once we determine where our place is, we should use our opportunities to grow and gain knowledge to perform our duties within that place. I am writing with the belief that God wants us to be the best we can be. He wants us to learn and gain knowledge and wisdom. I believe that if we don't use it, we lose it.

Chance, as mentioned in this title, is a gambling situation in which you need luck to win the prize: no skill involved, no preparation, no special knowledge and with no control on the outcome.

Choices are intentional: decisive determinations that are made by recognizing your opportunities and capabilities. Choice is fulfilled by preparation and accomplished through action.

Your destiny is where you're meant to be. I believe that everyone's destiny is where their recognized abilities and actions take them. You cannot be a doctor without the proper preparation (educational studies and on the job training). If your destiny were to become a doctor, then you would fail if you choose not to go to medical school. You might say, "It must not be my destiny to become a doctor," possibly so, but do not use this as an excuse for laziness.

If your choices lead you to inadequacy in your life, then I believe you need to make other choices and change your destiny. Choices that lead to good family relationships, good home, a good spiritual family, financial stability, and love of spouse are choices that lead you to a proper destiny.

Again, if you're headed down a road of uncertainty and depending on "chance" to find your way, then you must change course now. Make a choice - an intentional choice, setting in motion a series of events that will lead you to your proper destiny. It is not by chance that you get to Heaven.

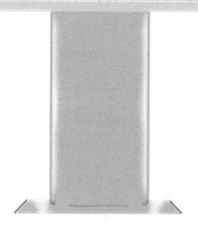

A CANDLE
LOOSES NO LIGHT
BY LIGHTING
ANOTHER CANDLE.

Is your candle burning? Or should I ask if you are letting your "life" shine to the world around you? If the choices you have made in life have resulted in family unity, spiritual understanding, and the confidence that faith in God gives you, your candle is burning and I suggest you shine your light. You are blessed and people need to see your candle burning. Sharing your light within your family, neighbors, workplace, community and the world is a witness to your life—lighting your candle. The impact of lighting another's candle, by making positive changes in their life, creates a chain reaction: lighting many candles.

Lighting another's candle will make your light stronger by reflecting off those whom you have enlightened. There is an old folk song that I am sure everyone remembers, at least the chorus: "This little light of mine, I'm going to let it shine." The song goes on to say as we have received blessings we should let them shine so others can see.

It is something, as Christians, we are asked by Christ to do. We are to let our light shine and not hide it. Luke 11:33 tells us "No one, after lighting a lamp, puts it away in a cellar nor under a basket, but on the lampstand, so that those who enter may see the light." Luke 11:35 "See to it that the light within you is not darkness."

Your light shines through your personality. It is displayed through your smile, your deeds, your encouragement to others, and the sharing of your talents with others. It is seen in your eyes. Luke 11:34 "Your eye is the lamp of your body. When your eyes are good, your whole body also is full of light. But when they are bad, your body also is full of darkness." Keeping yourself full of light is the only way to have enough light to shine. The light of the earth is the sun, moon and stars. Just as they were placed here by God, the light of the spirit is placed within the believing Christian. Keeping pure in our belief, and demonstrating purity through our action, will create a light to shine.

In our business, Rhonda (my wife, best friend and business partner) and I believed that we should share knowledge with our staff by letting them know and learn as much as they wanted, in some cases more than they wanted. Many, in business, don't want to teach their staff for fear of loosing them to their competition. We practiced the concept, "It is better to train your staff and loose them, than not train them and keep them." Untrained personnel do more harm than good for the business. Sharing knowledge is just one way of lighting others' candles.

Try touching your lit candle to another's unlit candle and see the difference it will make.

AS YOU GAIN WISDOM
YOU SPEAK LESS AND SAY MORE.

BETTER TO WEAR OUT
THAN TO RUST OUT.

BITTERNESS IS THE GREATEST BARRIER
BETWEEN YOU AND GOD.

CHRISTIANS NEVER
MEET FOR THE LAST TIME.

COME IN AND ALTAR YOUR LIFE.

"DO YOU KNOW WHERE YOU ARE GOING?"
GOD

DOING WHAT IS RIGHT TODAY
MEANS NO REGRETS TOMORROW.

DON'T CONFUSE FREE SPEECH
WITH LOOSE TALK.

DON'T COUNT THE THINGS YOU DO,
DO THE THINGS THAT COUNT.

AN INCH OF PROGRESS IS BETTER THAN A YARD OF GOOD INTENTIONS.

Intentions could be any goal that we intend to achieve. In this case, we are referring to "good intentions" - things we intend to do for the good of others. This one hits me hard. I have had many good intentions; they have not rewarded me, nor helped others. Intentions without actions are simply intentions. They are empty of feelings other than regret. It has been said when we get old and look back, we will have more things we regret not doing than things we regret doing.

Progress is the result of positive actions. Why do we not take action on our intentions? We make excuses, citing things that matter more, but do they? Sometimes this is as simple as selfishness. We need to have a servant's heart, not a self centered heart. If you see the smile of those whom we visit on cold gloomy days, you can see right away that your visit mattered a whole lot. To make progress we must make an effort to follow through with our intentions. We must be strong with a determination to follow through. We must use our resources to put into play those actions. We must be enthusiastic and ambitious, motivating ourselves to follow through with these good intentions.

How about intentions that would benefit ourselves? For example, we intend to go to church, but we choose to lie in bed instead. Would we choose staying in bed over a congregational meeting where Christ is present (Mathew 18:20)? Again, intentions have no reward unless action is taken. I wonder if we need to carry a list of our intentions to St. Peter, or if God knows of our intentions. How will he grade them? Will he say, "He meant to go see his mother more and I will give him credit for those intentions" or maybe God canceled the good intentions because he heard a mother praying, "Take me for I am so lonely."

The road to Hell is paved with good intentions. What does this mean? Who said it? The meaning is clear. As to who said it...I have found no solid reference, but the words hit home hard. It never hurts to repeat to ourselves these words in order to push us into action.

Maybe we should write down our intentions as we would write down our goals. Make a list and check them off. Put them in order of importance keeping our "heart open" as we do this prioritizing. As we make this list, I want to remind you there are four major categories to use as a guide in setting the right things first:

1.   ... both important and urgent.
2.   ...urgent but not important.
3.   ...important but not urgent.
4.   ...neither important nor urgent.

With our hearts open, we can determine the truly important things and make them urgent.

Intentions (good intentions) are a good beginning. They show that our heart is in the right place. However, the rewards of those intentions are not realized until the actions to achieve those intentions are taken; this is progress.

ANY WHO
ANGERS YOU,
CONQUERS YOU.

Tiger and Pepé were enjoying treats from Rhonda's grandmother when Tiger felt that she had given Pepé one extra treat. He became angry and left the room to show his anger. He then failed to get any more treats. We react, many times, like Tiger in this story. We let others anger us, ending with negative results. Anger takes over the brain and the results are never beneficial to the decision making faculty.

Don't disrupt your decision making capabilities with anger. Be wiser and smarter than to allow this to happen. When you allow others to anger you, they have won the battle and have reduced the control of your own decision making; therefore, they have gained control over you. Your decision making becomes revenge (negative). "A fool gives full vent to his anger, but a wise man keeps himself under control" (Proverbs 29:11). Remember, use kindness rather than anger. "A gentle answer turns away wrath, but a harsh word stirs up anger" (Proverbs 15:1).

When we are angry, we usually say harsh things. "But now you must rid yourselves of all such things as these: anger, rage, malice, slander and filthy language from your lips" (Colossians 3:8).

In the Old Testament, anger was something that was feared. This was the wrath of God (retribution for sin). God used fear for control and an attention getting effect. As I see it, we as humans, do not have the authority to use anger in this way. In the New Testament, we are taught that anger is something we are to refrain from. "'In your anger do not sin': Do not let the sun go down while you are still angry" (Ephesians 4:26). Anger, when displayed by us, is negative toward the purpose of Christian endeavors: "for man's anger does not bring about the righteous life that God desires" (James 1:20).

Respond with kindness: the greatest weapon with which to attack anger. By rejecting anger you stay in control, maintaining your faculties and pleasing God.

B. I. B. L. E.
BASIC
INSTRUCTION
BEFORE
LEAVING
EARTH.

What instructions do you need to leave this earth? Assuming you are either going to Heaven or Hell, you would need the "how to" to arrive at your choice. The best source for this knowledge is the Bible. Leaving earth is such a permanent thing (there is no going back for a second chance), you would definitely want to know how to depart properly. Time and effort for proper instructions would be a top priority issue. First, let's see where we want to go when we leave earth. Heaven seems to be the place I would choose. The itinerary for heaven looks better than that for hell. As in any good destination, the difficulty and investment is greater for heaven than hell. Mathew 7:13-14 tells us that the gate is wide to hell and narrow to Heaven. I feel, however, even though the instructions to arrive at Heaven are clear, they sometimes seem to be argumentative. My aim is on the bull's eye: keeping the most important things the most important things. The incidentals that are heard as controversial are more worship choices than salvation choices. I tend to treat them as such. My salvation is a gift from God and something that is promised. We must realize that salvation and eternal life are gifts from God (Ephesians 2:8): not earned nor given as a reward, but are gifts (grace). But, even a gift must be opened to be realized. To open the gift of salvation, you must pass a qualifying examination. The failing grade for this examination is Hell. With the consequences being so extreme, it would be very important to read and study the manual. I have found the instructions are not as simple as "1, 2, 3", but there are some definite qualifications: hear, believe, repent, confess, and be baptized- receiving the gift of the Holy Spirit.

First, the most obvious, you must believe in God and that heaven and hell do exist. To believe this, you must hear the account of the facts contained in the Bible and specifically those pertaining to the biblical plan of salvation.

Philip and the Ethiopian eunuch (Acts 8:26-40) give a glimpse of the need to be taught (hear) about salvation. It tells more than hearing: it tells of the action needed (baptism). Through studying and hearing we must make a choice to believe (Mark 16:16) in God, believe in Jesus Christ and accept the cross as our means of salvation (faith). We must accept the crucifixion of Christ - accept the offer of salvation. Repent of our sins and confess that Jesus is the Son of God (Luke 13:3).

Romans 10:9 tells us that we must confess with our mouth that Jesus is Lord. I take this to mean aloud (verbally) and having others to hear- witnesses, so to speak, acknowledging to others that we believe. When being baptized, we will be asked to verbally acknowledge (confess) that Jesus is the Son of God and that his death on the cross was for the remission of our sins. We must accept the death of our past and be born anew. Repent of our sins (be sorry for our sins and transgressions) and begin to change our actions and habits.

It is here we receive the hope of eternal life and the rewards of Heaven. This hope is something that I have difficulty explaining. It is hope, yet it is firmly promised: there is no doubt. A guarantee you might say. It is only hope because it is unseen. The best explanation that I have heard is "confident expectations." I know I am in the book of life because I have been promised. I don't hope this, but it is the hope of this that fulfills my life and gives me peace. How can I feel so confident that I am in the book of life? This may sound arrogant on my part, but let me tell you why I feel this way. Salvation is an individual thing. Each of us has been given the free will to choose our salvation. The instruction manual tells us many things that lead us to salvation. Even though they are not in the same paragraph of text, they are inspired by God through the Holy Spirit (2 Timothy 3:16). This is why I choose the plan of salvation: hear, believe, repent, confess, and be baptized. If I have done all these things and continue to live with Christ in my heart, then I have been promised salvation and the Kingdom of Heaven (confident expectations). It is not because I am perfect, but because I have opened God's gift and continue to cherish it. Having joy and peace, along with the "God within feeling", is a spiritual thing and part of my knowing of my place in Heaven. I think some fight this spiritual feeling: afraid of showing spiritual exaggeration and fear of persecution. You must believe you have a place in Heaven just as you believe there is a Heaven.

What do I gain here on earth from these confident expectations (hope)? I have peace within; I share my life with God; I have joy in my life; there are fruits of my labor; I have received all of God's promises of life (blessings) and I do not fear death. I have said this many times, but with an additional phrase that goes like this: "I do not fear death; however, I won't do anything to encourage it." This is living hope. Now remember, I have difficulty explaining hope. How do you explain hope that you are experiencing now? "It just is." Let's just say that it is living within us as Christ is living within us. Hope, joy, love, peace, and the Holy Spirit are all living within those who have withstood the test of salvation. Those who have followed the instructions of the manual are blessed with the grace of God through their faith.

Warning – Improper use of this life could lead to eternal damnation. These instructions must be followed for salvation to be realized. Improper use of this manual (Bible) could cause damage. Failure to follow the manual's warning and instructions can result in severe personal injury. The manual doesn't say hearing only will get you to heaven, nor believing only, nor repenting only, nor baptism only but it mentions all favorably. So why, why would I not want to follow these powerful suggestions.

GIVE SATAN AN INCH
AND HE WILL BECOME THE RULER.

GOD CAN HEAL A BROKEN HEART
BUT HE HAS TO HAVE ALL THE PIECES.

GOD GIVES WHAT'S RIGHT,
NOT WHAT'S LEFT.

GOD GRADES US ON THE CROSS...
NOT THE CURVE.

GOD'S HAMMER CAN SMASH
THE HARDEST HEART.

HE WHO THROWS DIRT...
LOOSES GROUND.

HEAVEN— ALL GAIN ... NO PAIN.

HELL: TRUTH SEEN TOO LATE.

HOME IMPROVEMENT PROJECT...
BRING YOUR FAMILY TO CHURCH.

BE KIND...

EVERYONE IS

FIGHTING A BATTLE.

The population of the United States has just reached 300 million. This means there are about 300 million individual battles being fought. Some of the battles will be larger than others. Nevertheless, they are occupying the mind and presenting challenges that affect the daily activity of these individuals. Understanding that, I would ask that we think before we react to small incidents. Rather than taking an adversarial approach to these situations, we could express concern and possibly turn them into opportunities. Many times, discovering and helping with others battles, will help us as well.

I believe there could be another side to the story. Possibly, there are three sides to the story: my side, your side and the side of reason. This "side of reason" would be what an outside observer might see. Many times we only look at the one side, our side. This reminds me of a song by Toby Keith entitled *I Want to Talk About Me*. But, we must remember that God made this world for all and not just for me.

Sometimes, when Rhonda and I are traveling, across country or simply commuting locally from one place to another, we will be discussing a situation within our family. Then, we will notice each individual house along the roadway and Rhonda will say..."You know, the people in each of those homes are dealing with some type of situation." There are people dealing with death, addictions, injury, loss of jobs, divorce, among many other calamities. In most cases, much greater battles than ours are being experienced. This puts our particular problem in perspective.

When growing up, our family struggled with many battles. Possibly, this is why I feel so strong about understanding the other side. We are so quick to judge without understanding the circumstances. One can overcome these adversities, and a kind word goes a long way in helping. The underlying reasons are somewhat ignored when our own life activities are disrupted by the acts of others, such as someone cutting us off in traffic, making a simple mistake with our order, or putting too much starch on our shirts. These are just a few of the many daily activities where someone does not perform as we feel they should. One could think these acts were intentional and to harm us personally. I ask that we would give them the benefit of the doubt. The reason being, we don't know the whole story, the other side.

Battles are fought daily - some are won and some are lost. Be generous with your kindness. We never know if people have just won or just lost or just discovered their battle.

Life not only happens to us, but to others as well. What if we stop and think before we react?

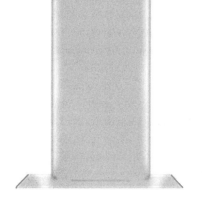

BE KNOWN FOR
YOUR DEEDS
NOT YOUR MORTGAGES.

According to The *American Heritage Dictionary*, the history of the word mortgage comes from Old French "mort" meaning dead and from German "gage" meaning pledge. This means that the early form of the word was "dead pledge." This makes a mortgage somewhat negative. One is forced to mortgage, basically, because he is not expected to act good on a promise. Deeds, on the other hand, are done with positive connotation. Positive because of what they do for both the giver and receiver.

We are not talking about the deed you get to show ownership in property, but the deed you do for someone. What have we done that we could say, "I've done my good deed today"? Every day gives us the opportunity to do good deeds. Sometime we pass it up. Possibly because we are so busy. What would be my epitaph? Will it say he was known for his deeds, or will it say he was known for his promises?

Sometimes deeds appear small to you but mean so much to the recipient. Contemplating what we could do for someone in need is not a deed. I have been guilty of this many times. I have talked to myself, in an effort to improve in this area, and concluded... to do something is better than to do nothing. Sometimes it just takes words or offering a hand. It matters not the size of the deed, just the act.

As a doer of deeds, what we get in return is often greater than the deed itself. The gratitude seen in the face of the recipient touches our heart. This glowing expression is our reward and it raises our level of love. God is smiling. We should say thank you for giving us an opportunity.

Are we a good receiver of deeds? I have struggled with this most of my life. I have not been a good receiver of deeds. Whatever the reason, I now choose to receive with only thanksgiving in my heart. No more trying to reason why they would do such a deed or how I can repay it. I just will accept it and pass it on. The one thing that made me change: I was taking pleasure away from the giver when I received gifts or deeds reluctantly. I now chose to accept with the same love in which it was given. The opportunities abound to "pass it on."

BEFORE YOU TRY TO KEEP UP WITH YOUR NEIGHBOR... SEE WHERE HE IS GOING.

Who is our neighbor? According to the Encarta Dictionary a neighbor is somebody who lives or is located nearby... on the same street or in the same town. It continues to describe neighbor as being very close to something or somebody. It is according to whom we are talking and to what reference we have to label someone a neighbor. If we are talking about the State of Tennessee, we could say Kentucky is our neighbor to the north. It is obvious that, on this marquee, we are not talking about our neighbor being a state. I believe with this marquee, we are referring to an acquaintance, a near relative, a friend, or one that can even be characterized as of an undefined relationship. It is quite obvious that God places a very high regard for our neighbors: "to love your neighbor" is preceded only by "to love God" as Jesus refers to this in Matthew 22:37-39.

But back to the question, who is your neighbor? From what I can ascertain, your neighbor can be the person living next door or miles away. It is all relative. Neighbor is more relationship oriented than geographical oriented. When asked this question "Who is my neighbor?" Jesus uses the parable of the Good Samaritan to identify a good neighbor (Luke 10:25-27). In this case, the Samaritan was the good neighbor and he did not even know his neighbor. But, Jesus' point was to define a neighbor.

What do we know about our neighbor? There are no doubt bad neighbors as well. They would be the ones who ignore the many instructions and admonitions concerning neighbors that are found in God's teachings. Neighbors with characteristics described as selfish, inconsiderate, irresponsible, and unruly might be called a bad neighbor.

Why are we following the example set by our neighbor? We must remember that we can be the neighbor or we can be the "neighboree" (I realize this is not a legitimate word, but I couldn't find one more appropriate). For the neighbors who neither follows nor lead, I would call the abstainers. They neither set examples nor follow examples. As a neighbor, we can be put into one of these categories or positions: follow, lead or abstain. We may not realize our "neighbor" position. But, it is probably one of the most important positions for the pursuit of a Christ like attitude. Whether we are influencing or being influenced, being a good neighbor has a great impact on lives: ours and our neighbors.

I am fortunate; I have great neighbors, the ones next door and the ones far away. I would describe a good neighbor as one who gives help before help is needed - one who displays concern and takes action. Not all of my neighbors have the same spiritual beliefs. But, being a neighbor has other defining characteristics (such as serving those in need) that are not parted by minuscule differences in spiritual beliefs. By minuscule beliefs, I mean beliefs that should not cause argumentative nor invasive actions toward one another, whether within our spiritual, occupational, family or physical paradigm. Neighborly neighbors get along and find joy within their neighborhood.

We should understand our choices in life. We should understand that others influence those choices. We should search our soul to determine whether we choose to accept or reject those influences...thus the choice. We follow because someone is leading and something is usually missing in our lives. Who we follow is the greatest decision we can make. Let's think about this for a second. Let's not act too quickly. If you neighbor has something you like or admire or does something that you see yourself doing, you must think for a second and analyze the situation. Sometimes all is not what it appears. I see people with enormous homes, fancy automobiles, who take expensive vacations, and wear expensive cloths and as they say in that commercial...they're in debt up to their eyeballs. Know the whole story before you try to keep up.

Follow the wise. You need to know whom you're trying to keep up with. A little introspection would help you determine whom to follow or not to follow. It makes sense to follow the wise neighbor - the one with the balanced approach to life, the one who has respect from fellow neighbors, and a loving family and spiritual family. It is ok not to try to keep up at all. Possibly, you should be the one to set the example.

Whatever you do, set your own sights based upon sound and prudent judgment. Have a plan and know where you and your family are going.

BEHIND THE CLOUDS
THE SUN IS
ALWAYS SHINNING.

I will never forget my first airplane flight. As the clouds were quickly approaching, I anticipated with wonder what going through these clouds would be like. Would it be like hitting a soft pillow of shaving cream or maybe like crashing through a wall of smoke? From the underside, the clouds were dark and dreary, but once we reached the other side, I looked back at one of the most beautiful sights I had ever seen. The sun was shining on a fluffy bed of glistening cotton. I wanted to stare out the window and absorb all the wonder. The brighter side was entirely different from the darker side. It made me forget that it was raining down below.

The cloud analogy could be translated into something that depresses you: sickness, a bad relationship, a problem at work, or anything that creates stress or trauma. You must realize that things happen, and we must respond to those things with hope. Just as my flying experience revealed the sun above the clouds, we must look past problems, sickness, or bad relationships to see life without these issues. This is the first step in desiring change: realizing that things are capable of being better. If our minds can see the sunshine behind the clouds, our minds can make choices that will get us beyond those clouds.

Our mind is the strength of our existence and should be used liberally. Our mind can see beyond the clouds if given the opportunity. It will be hard at times; it will be heart breaking at times, but you have the power, through determination, developed by your own brainpower. You must realize that the calamity can be dealt with properly, allowing the sun to be seen. If we can have that hope and understand that life happens and we must deal with it, then we can determine the outcome through the choices we make. Don't forget you can ask for help from friends and from God through prayer. Sometimes it may seem the sun will never shine again, but remember it is just above the clouds. You simply need something to take you through those clouds.

It takes a very optimistic person to see the sun above the clouds. I have written many times in this book about having a positive mental attitude. I want to emphasize that I believe a positive mental attitude is a choice. If you think you have a negative attitude, I encourage you to change. If you want to see the sun behind the clouds, you must have a positive outlook. A negative attitude can only be changed by doing and thinking differently than you are doing or thinking now. Remember, if you react to things negatively, it is very difficult to see the sun behind the clouds. In fact, you don't believe the sun is behind the clouds.

Believing that the sun is there is like believing that the Son is there. There is evidence of both and our choices will determine our future. Choose Christ and choose the Son.

LOST? FREE DIRECTIONS INSIDE.

MOST PEOPLE ARE WILLING TO SERVE GOD BUT ONLY IN AN ADVISORY CAPACITY.

NO MATTER WHAT HAPPENS, THERE IS ALWAYS SOMEONE WHO KNEW IT WOULD.

NOTHING RUINS THE TRUTH LIKE STRETCHING IT.

ONE LOOKING FOR GOD... IS NOT LOST.

ONE WEEK WITHOUT PRAYERS MAKES ONE WEAK.

OUR PAST SHOULD BE A SPRINGBOARD ... NOT A HAMMOCK.

OUR PRESENT CHOICE DETERMINES OUR FUTURE REWARDS.

PATIENCE IS A VIRTUE THAT CARRIES A LOT OF WAIT.

BETTER TO
WEAR OUT
THAN TO RUST OUT.

Rhonda and I like to cruise. I have noticed that the ship's maintenance staff is constantly painting sections of the hull. When you arrive into a port it is easy to see which ships are well taken care of and which ones are neglected. The neglected ones are all rusty and look old. The same thing can happen to us as human beings. Not that we must paint ourselves up, but we are constantly in need of maintenance to keep from getting rusty.

The adage "use it or lose it" comes to mind. The more we use our body and its muscles, the more strength and endurance we will have. I don't need to prove this because it has already been proven. We just keep ignoring it as a fact. Healthy living includes some type of physical exercise. Choose yours or rust out.

The body has limitations that must be kept in mind when exercising. We should all check with our doctor to know how much we should exercise. But, the theory of the heart having only so many beats is untrue. In fact, my brother-in-law is (OOPS, I almost told his age)...well, let's say his body's condition is considerably younger than his actual age. The point is: he exercises daily and has a resting heartbeat of 54 beats per minute, taking no medication. His father died as a young man. He decided to respond to this heredity issue. Keeping a positive attitude, he has built a stronger body. This didn't occur overnight, and it took years of maintenance.

Our minds have similar muscles, with lack of use, they too will shrink and deteriorate. Studies have shown the brain has been able to strengthen itself. I know we have all heard forgetting is inevitable, but I disagree. The more you exercise the brain, the less forgetful you become. Of course, there are diseases that strip us of our minds, but studies show exercising the mind even reduces the effect of these diseases. We don't forget: we just misplace the file. Mental exercises will help us find it. I believe some feel that we will blow a fuse if we fill the brain too full. In reality, you cannot fill it. God gave us more gigabytes in the brain than the largest computer on earth.

Whatever you do today you see the results tomorrow:

Exercise today
tomorrow your body is stronger.

Study today
tomorrow your knowledge is greater.

Play today
tomorrow your disposition is better.

Worship today
tomorrow your faith is stronger.

Work today
tomorrow your wealth is greater.

Rest today
tomorrow your body will be recovered.

Eat healthy today
tomorrow your body begins to heal.

It is simply the rule of cause and effect: action – result.

What is this doing on a church marquee? It reiterates that God wants us to be all that we can be.

The healthier, more active we are, both physically and mentally, the more we can help in God's plan. After all, many Bible characters were old and active. Methuselah lived 969 years and had children after 782 years (Genesis 5:26-27).   He must have kept himself in pretty good shape.

BY PATIENCE,
THE SNAIL REACHED
THE ARK.

Wonderful things can happen with the simple act of having patience. Wisdom, understanding, hope and healing can be gained. Let us not fail to mention that we are meeting God's desires when we liberally apply patience. We don't know how long it took the snail to reach the ark, but we can imagine it took quite a while because we know that snails move at a very slow pace. By reaching the ark the snail gave his species life. The lesson here is obvious: it is important to reach your destination, not the speed in which you reach it. Do not be impatient or give up; Philippians 4:6 "Do not be anxious about anything, but in everything, by prayer and petition, with thanksgiving, present your requests to God." Any worthwhile goal takes time. I've heard that you can eat an elephant one bite at a time. I don't know who wants to eat an elephant, but the job could be done with patience. Huge jobs can be completed by spending 15 minutes a day, but this takes patience.

It has been said that the "now" generation is an instant generation and does not have the ability of what has been labeled as "delayed gratification." I believe you have it or don't have it, because of the choices you make, not by what one generation has or has not. After all, it is individual choices that determine what a generation does or does not do. I believe patience is a virtue and should be desired. If it is desired and you "have not," then you must learn. To learn patience is like anything else— "practice makes perfect.

The first thing I think of is how you can buy an automobile of enormous cost based on the ability to make the monthly payment. This is a prime example of instant gratification. Can you actually afford this? Your grandfather would say no. I can understand that you possibly could not afford to pay cash for an automobile, especially early in life, but we buy the most expensive allowed to make the monthly payment. We later catch ourselves short of cash due to an emergency. Would it not be prudent to get a lesser automobile now and save some extra for emergencies? Save the difference and, with compounded interest, it would be there the next time you needed another automobile. This same concept is applicable to houses, furniture, electronics, vacations, etc.

Delayed gratification will still get you there with security and with the satisfaction of God's desires being met. We are stewards of all things here on earth. All things belong to God. I certainly believe God wants us to have nice things, but I think that he also wants us to be responsible and earn those nice things. After all, when we borrow for those things, we have not earned them. It used to be low brow to borrow money, but now it is apropos to everyday life. Like many things, too much debt is not good. Debt sometimes controls our life and adds stress to relationships. Financial issues are the number one cause of marital problems today. How can a Christian society embrace debt when it adds so much stress to our lives? You can avoid this with patience. This is just one example of patience. Many other life situations can be altered to a more favorable outcome when approached with patience.

Patience can be developed through choice. I feel with hope (the promise given by Christ for eternal salvation), patience becomes more endurable. Hope obtained through faith establishes the desire and fortitude to live the life necessary to receive God's promise (Hebrews 6:11).

Thoughts Behind The Words

PRAYER
WILL GIVE
YOU A
CALM-PLEX.

A BURDEN MUST BE CARRIED BEFORE IT CAN BE PUT DOWN.

My interpretation of this statement indicates that burdens are not necessarily a bad thing. In "life," some burdens must be carried to fulfill a responsibility. The definition of a burden indicates it must be carried—"Something that is carried." Life is not easy, but the results of burdens can be enormously beneficial to the character building process.

We can also look at others' burdens and grow from them. For example, "the greatest burden" (Jesus bearing the burden of the cross), was a burden given to Christ from the very beginning and was carried out so that all could receive the gift of eternal life. As we learn from this example of a burden, sacrifice is sometimes necessary and rewards follow.

Many of the burdens I speak of are burdens that I have experienced in my life. Sure they are real, but I am not referring to the greater burdens, such as the death of a child, physical abuse, torture, cancer or some other terrifying disease. I can only imagine how difficult an experience of this magnitude must be. These burdens require the help of a greater power to overcome. Many prisoners of war have indicated they would not have been able to sustain the abuse and torture if not by believing and turning to God for comfort and courage to endure. But, even though I have not endured such horrific burdens, I do call upon God to help me through the smaller ones and constantly search for the opportunity reveled by these burdens.

We must help others, if necessary, to carry their burdens. The ones we love are many times burdened and our responsibility lies in helping with their burden. This means sometimes other's burdens will become our burdens (Galatians 6:1-5).

Don't let our burdens get us down. God will not give us more burdens than we can bear. He also offers us help, through prayer: (Psalm 55:22) "Cast your cares on the Lord and he will sustain you; he will never let the righteous fall."

How do we put down our burdens? By laying them at the feet of Jesus and calling on Him for strength and comfort: (Mt 11:28) "Come to me, all you who are weary and burdened, and I will give you rest."

Putting down our burdens could be as simple as doing the things that are expected of us— completing the task necessary, transforming the burden to a blessing. Many times a burden may turn into an opportunity. Pray that we recognize this and follow through with the opportunities given us. We must ask God, through prayer, for his help to endure. But, our greatest benefit is to overcome the burden and strengthen our character.

Define your life situations as burdens or opportunities. Sometimes it is hard to determine the difference. Again, I am not speaking of the "Big Ones," but many burdens are camouflaged opportunities. They offer challenges: when completed, growth in knowledge and wisdom is gained. Don't create burdens when they don't exist; accept the challenges and turn them into opportunities. Carefully control your thoughts through a positive mental attitude with a positive outlook.

When is it our burden? It belongs to us when it is our responsibility to take action: when our moral and spiritual beliefs tell us that action must be taken.

Burdens are life's way of expressing itself.

THIS CHURCH
IS PRAYER CONDITIONED.

TO BELITTLE
IS TO BE LITTLE.

TOO MUCH TIME IS WASTED BY PEOPLE
TELLING HOW BUSY THEY ARE.

TRIALS SHOULD MAKE YOU FEEL BETTER...
NOT BITTER.

VOTE FOR THE CONSERVATIVE
OF YOUR CHOICE.

WELL DONE
IS BETTER THAN WELL SAID.

WHATEVER YOU DISLIKE IN ANOTHER PERSON
BE SURE TO CORRECT IN YOURSELF.

"WILL THE ROAD THAT YOU ARE ON GET YOU
TO MY PLACE?"
GOD

CIRCUMSTANCES NEVER CREATE CHARACTER... THEY REVEAL IT.

Do you respond or react to certain conditions in which you have no control or are beyond your control?   We will call these conditions circumstances. Do you show good character? The character we are referring to is "moral or ethical strength."

Do you react or respond? If we were a patient and we were given treatment for an illness, and we react, it probably would have an adverse effect on our health or our condition: being negative. If we respond, we would begin improvement and this would be positive. We want to respond positively to circumstances. This simply requires a thought process that directs you to respond rather than react. Our goal is a positive outcome. If we react (negatively) each and every time we are tempted, then our character is diminished. Character is built by one response at a time or destroyed by one reaction at a time.

Character goes a long way in determining your future. Some of the things that fall under the character umbrella are: trust, responsibility, compassion, faith, family, and the company that we keep. It is easy to see that all these characteristics favor success. According to Steven Covey's *The 7 Habits of Highly Effective People*, those in the top five percentile of highly effective people have these characteristics. I would place my character among one of the most valued attributes of my life.

As we build our character, it is important to do things that are constructive to a "good character" and avoid those that are destructive. We start by making choices and talking to ourselves, asking questions and answering in a way that leads in moral and ethical directions. Remember the "Golden Rule"... "Do unto others as you would have them do unto you." Stick to this rule, no exceptions, and your brain will be filled with moral decision making characteristics.

How you handle circumstances reveals your character. If you catch yourself angry and show this with emotions, these emotional displays determine the way others perceive your character. Some would argue that this is your true character. I believe, even though it may be your given character, you can change, or if not change, you can control it to a more desired outcome. Your communication to yourself must be constant in order to make a change. Put yourself in the position of others who would be judging your character, and change your actions accordingly. I believe your displayed character can be learned and controlled to a more desired character, thereby forming a habit.

I can only emphasize the importance of character building through our actions. Our actions, in every situation, reveal our character. Being concerned with our actions shows a desire to be of good character. That is important to our destiny and is what God desires in us. "Even a child is known by his actions, by whether his conduct is pure and right" (Proverbs 20:11).

The Holy Bible teaches good character. Read it for instructions.

Thoughts Behind The Words

WAL-MART IS NOT
THE ONLY
SAVING PLACE.

COME INSIDE
FOR A FAITH LIFT.

It is not surgery. It is not painful at all. In fact, it is quite gratifying. It is always refreshing to hear the word taught, studied and expressed. Some of these teachings open our minds to explore new avenues that we might not have thought of before. We need to keep our minds open to the scriptures to enlighten ourselves daily, refraining from the dogmatic approach that sometimes blinds us from facts and truth. Some of which are just traditions or false truths that have been learned without full knowledge. Focus, in any Christian based congregation, should be on the love of Christ with a heart for Bible based teachings. Any good teacher will continue learning, sharing what they have learned with the students.

When life takes us away from those who share the love of Christ, socially separating us from other Christians, it can stretch the spiritual line thin and lower our faith level. This desertion or spiritual laziness can lead to faith deterioration.

We gain so much in so many ways when we attend church services. If you think you hear the same thing every time you go, I suggest you have an input and voice your opinion. If you are rejected without cause or explanations... change congregations. I believe that everyone has questions. They need to be answered spiritually with an attitude of a teacher. The Bible may never be completely understood and agreed upon, but continuous study reveals new thoughts each time it is read. An encouraging attribute of reading and studying any book is that it inspires learning and encourages understanding.

The lifting of our faith can mean different things to different people. There are those who have never found Christ. For those, finding Christ would be a wonderful lift. They may have never been exposed to church, so if we could only get them inside we could tell them about Christ, but it is not that simple. There is a built-in "brake" applied every time we mention church to those who have never been. We must give them a taste of what it is all about by exposing them to our Christ-loving attitudes at the workplace and other social gatherings.

Think of ten ways to show your Christian faith to those around you. Here are some possible ways: courtesy when driving, smiles, refraining from bad language, invitations to service, concern for others (with actions), visiting in hospital, food when ill, listening to problems, help with scheduling at work, encouragement, answering questions about religion, etc. There are many who do not go to church that do these good things. Just make sure that as a Christian we do them also.

If we have grown lax in our Christian activities, we, too, may need a faith lift.

FOOLISH MEN THINK ABOUT TALKING ... WISE MEN TALK ABOUT THINKING.

Being able to talk about "what you are thinking," without being shut out or being labeled a critic or enemy, is a talent of the wise. You must be able to talk about your thoughts and ideas in order to transfer knowledge and wisdom to or from others. As I mentioned in my preface, very few ever have an original thought. If we don't talk about thinking, we will not get an idea that will generate new thought. It is like priming the pump, if anyone knows what that means.

I believe wise men listen with comprehension - trying to understand the viewpoint or basis for the message given, rather than with adversity. It is important to find all point of views in order to determine the proper understanding of any issue. To talk about issues of importance, with this goal in mind, is how wise men become wise men. Without open conversation in political, religious, occupational, and historical arenas, we would at some point find pandemonium - no consensus, no compromises nor understanding of others' ideas, beliefs or opinions. It takes several peoples' ideas to form a single opinion that is appropriate for a majority. Before you criticize, it is necessary to keep others' perspective in mind. It is important to think, but it is important to think aloud - letting others know of the process and help those listening to understand the thought process of the wise.

You must listen to a wise man. No wisdom will be gained unless you listen. Wise men first listen to gain wisdom; therefore, setting the perpetual motion that will create wise men from wise men. We are not all born wise.

I believe one should be able to talk about issues with no fear of criticism other than constructive criticism. I would suggest that you receive and give criticism with the same gentleness. If your goal is to grow, you must receive criticism with a positive attitude, keeping your anger at bay. I believe this is the only way to talk about thinking.

The foolish, as mentioned in this marquee, are speaking only to entertain themselves, having very little in a productive nature to say. But they are always trying to be the one talking, so they must always be thinking of something to say rather than listening to what others are saying.

Anytime we are engaged in conversation that encourages thinking, it is good for the growth of the brain. Thinking conversation mobilizes the receptors of the mind to stimulate activity and expand its capabilities. We should encourage ourselves to join in conversations that require thinking and in activities that also encourage thinking. I don't know of a one of us who could not use some growth in the brain area.

Gaining wisdom also helps you gain knowledge: because the wise seek knowledge. A wise man once told me that to gain knowledge you must be taught. My personal example is witnessed in my weak grammar. I have been blessed that Rhonda has a good understanding of grammar. But, I wanted to improve my understanding so I purchased a book on grammar for third graders and began to catch up. It's amazing ... I have already argued with the book. But, I am beginning to learn the importance of proper grammar. It makes me think, I then can talk to Rhonda about thinking. But, it was not until I gained wisdom that I found the proper direction in learning grammar. This direction came with an epiphany during the night. I have been telling people things to do and things not to do with expectations of them accepting them as truths: thinking they would begin immediately to change

56

their life. All of a sudden, I realized that I was rejecting information from those who were directing me in an area that I knew very little about. I began to see the same frustration on their faces as I have had when I was the one with the frustration. This epiphany (tipping point) has changed and will continue to change my life.

Let's listen when we should be listening, talk when we should be talking and not forget to talk about things that we think about.

PRAYER– UNLIMITED MINUTES,
NO ROAMING CHARGES,
COMPLETE COVERAGE.

PRAYER– USE ANYWHERE,
USE ANYTIME,
ALWAYS CONNECTED.

READ THE BIBLE DAILY.
PREVENT TRUTH DECAY.

SALVATION IS FREE...
BUT THE PRICE WASN'T CHEAP.

SIGN BROKEN.
MESSAGE INSIDE THIS SUNDAY.

SOME MINDS ARE LIKE CONCRETE...
ALL MIXED UP AND SET PERMANENTLY.

SOME PEOPLE WILL BELIEVE ANYTHING
IF IT IS WHISPERED TO THEM.

SUCCESS PROCEEDS WORK
ONLY IN THE DICTIONARY.

GOD ANSWERS PRAYERS WITH YES, NO, OR WAIT.

When we pray, we need to be prepared to accept God's answer. I think sometimes we fit into a plan and our prayer may not be answered the way we desire. We are confused because we may not see or fully understand the plan. However, I believe that not all things fit into a larger plan. Some things happen because we make stupid choices. I also believe we can influence God's decision with prayer. I believe God is a loving God; with prayers that are made with a believing heart, He will consider our desires to the point of "changing or altering his plan" to grant our wishes. I must believe this because the word tells me this. Some things are just "life happenings" and our prayers concerning those things, I definitely believe, will be considered most favorable in God's answer. I believe that how we pray, who is praying and how many are praying have an effect on the answer. But, those prayers that are answered unfavorably or seemed unanswered give us no reason to place blame on anyone or anything, especially God. It must be considered that the prayer is answered with no or wait. God does not punish with unanswered prayers.

Maybe there is something we don't know. Many times things happen that we don't understand despite our many prayers. These are tragic things happening to good people, and we just shake our heads with questionable understanding. We think God didn't hear our prayers because He would not have let something this tragic happen with our prayers asking otherwise. The only possible explanation we have is that he answered the prayers with no, and this is hard to understand. Now we turn to the only solace we have: to trust that God is fulfilling a plan. A plan we may not see to fruition because life is too short. Or, we may not recognize nor understand the series of events that transpired to fulfill the plan, since we are too small to see or comprehend the big picture. But, we must realize that things happen, and these things affect other things; what happens today affects tomorrow, next year, next decade, the next century, and on and on till the end of time. I know I cannot see that far; but God can.

The Bible teaches us how to pray. Lessons from Christ on how to pray indicate we should get to the point and not pray just to hear ourselves or to "show off" our narrative talents: (Mathew 6:7) "And when you pray, do not keep on babbling like pagans, for they think they will be heard because of their many words." Prayer is to be short and to the point and from the heart. However, we should not pray hastily, (Ecclesiastes 5:2) "Do not be quick with your mouth, do not be hasty in your heart to utter anything before God. God is in heaven and you are on Earth, so let your words be few." I do appreciate those who can deliver a prayer, directed to God, where all the right words seem to flow and where all the issues are covered with understanding and meaning. I believe this is a talent realized.

I don't know of any specific instruction that indicates a prayer must be said aloud to be answered. However, I can definitely see a benefit of the prayer spoken aloud. If you are leading a congregational prayer, speaking aloud is mandatory so that the congregation may absorb and express the prayer to God as a group. When praying with someone for God's assistance to help with a particular situation ... to give a spiritual uplift - it is necessary to voice the prayer aloud.

Christ tells us to pray like this: (Mathew 6:9-13), "Our Father which art in heaven, Hallowed be thy name. Thy kingdom come, Thy will be done in earth, as it is in heaven. Give us this day our daily bread. And forgive us our debts, as we forgive our debtors. And lead us not into temptation, but deliver us from evil: For thine is the kingdom, and the power, and the glory, for ever. Amen" (King James Version).

Prayers need to be offered with determination and frequency. An event that needs prayers can contain many smaller events. For example, during the diagnosing, treatment and convalescing of any major medical event, prayers need to be expressed for such things as test, probes, emotions, travel, exploratory surgery, and many other things that are leading to and after any major treatment or surgery.

Prayer needs to be addressed with a sense of urgency and desirability: I want the outcome to be this or that. Our prayers are a direct line to God and should be voiced with specifics.

Prayers of thanksgiving - Most of my prayers are prayers of thanksgiving. I have been blessed in so many ways. I see those who are in worse shape than I and I pray (ask for Gods blessings) for them.

Miracle or not - We must recognize that our bodies are a temple, and what we do with them directly affects our performance. God gave us bodies, in his likeness, and I believe that is good. I will strive to take care of my body, both physically and mentally. God uses the healing power of our bodies, our knowledge and talents and the knowledge and talents of others to answer prayers. In many ways, it is a cooperative effort to answer prayers. We must do our part to complete this prayer answering achievement. If there is no action on our part, then the answer could be put on hold until we take that appropriate action. Through these efforts many prayers receive a yes answer. I believe these "yes answers" are, in essence, miracles. God uses many tools to answer our prayers. When we are in distress and offer a prayer and it is immediately answered, it is apparent that a supernatural power has intervened. This is also a miracle.

The Scriptures clearly indicate that believing is necessary to receive answered prayers (Matthew 21:22) "If you believe, you will receive whatever you ask for in prayer," (Mark 11:24) "Therefore I tell you, whatever you ask for in prayer, believe that you have received it, and it will be yours." We must be believers, have faith, and be in spirit to be among the loudest voices heard.

Open your heart when praying, be specific, and give thanks often.

GOD FEEDS THE BIRDS, BUT HE DOESN'T THROW THE SEEDS INTO THE NEST.

Everything we need, God provides. He provides food for the birds and every other animal on the planet. The point is that we do not need to fear survival. The source for food, clothing, shelter and many other needs and wants is abundant. The other point is that we must take action to get it.

Just as it is the responsibility of the bird to gather seeds for food, it is our responsibility to gather our "needs" from the resources provided. You very seldom see a hungry bird that is not digging and scratching for seeds, bugs and the like. We can learn a lot from the innate actions of these animals, such as survival through determination. Humans don't have this degree of "innate sense" determination that lower animals do. Sure we want to survive, but when the human's capabilities are measured and compared with other animals, we fall short.

We sometime take a statement like "God will provide" too far. For example, the fella that was stranded on his rooftop by rising flood waters, refused help from a neighbor with a canoe, saying "The Lord will take care of me." Sometime later, after the water had risen higher, another larger boat came by and begged him to get into the boat. The fella again repeated his reasoning, "The Lord will save me." Later, a helicopter came by and again the fella did not accept the ride. The flood took his life, and when approaching the gates of Heaven, he asked God why He had not saved him. God replied, "I tried; I sent two boats and a helicopter." This story is intended to show that God provides not only the resource, but the opportunity.

Even our salvation is our responsibility. God provides the resources and the instructions for our salvation, but it is up to us to find and accept it. If you are the least bit familiar with computers and computer programs, you know that you must check the box accepting the terms and conditions of the website or you don't get the download. We sometimes need to think about God's plan the same way ...we accept it, or we don't get it.

God does provide, but we must accept and gather it. Even when manna fell from the sky, it had to be gathered with terms and conditions.

We are the ones responsible for gathering the things that we need. It is through effort and willingness to achieve that we accomplish. If we don't...it's not God's fault... it is ours.

He will provide, but we must gather the "needs."

HAPPINESS

IS AN

INSIDE JOB.

We are constantly searching for happiness. We look to a bigger house, a nicer automobile, a computer with the most memory, a bigger TV, a longer vacation, or a certain job, among many other material things - to supply us with happiness. Yes, all these things can contribute to happiness, but we have all heard that money cannot buy happiness. I would agree there are many things that bring happiness which money will not buy. I also agree with Zig Ziglar, who made this statement in one of his seminars I attended: referring to money, he said, "I have lived with it, and I have lived without it, and believe me, it is better to live with it."

Is it more money that makes us happy? If while rubbing an Aladdin's lamp a genie appeared and gave us one wish, we would probably wish for money. We cannot depend on money alone to give us happiness. We should search for happiness before we search for money. If I could have only one - give me happiness.

If we felt money didn't make us happy, there would be no motivation for greater achievement, and we would be a regressive society. I don't think this would bring happiness either. But, sometimes, I feel we need a "capacity limit," so that we could dispose of the attitude "the more we have the more we want." This might make people look for the other things in life that also contribute to happiness.

Setting money and possessions aside, what does bring us happiness? Maybe, it's another person or our family, our love toward them and their love toward us. It could be a sporting event or an afternoon with friends. These are all good happiness givers. These ingredients in life are a positive influence and contribute to developing our "metabolism" for happiness.

We also need to feel secure in our faith and give cheerfully of our time and monies. Giving happiness is one way to receive happiness. This makes our soul happy and is yet another happiness ingredient in life.

All the things I have mentioned above are ingredients of a happy life. Only you have the power to control these things, and your attitude will be the ultimate test of your happiness. If you stop and count your blessings, you will begin to realize that happiness is all in the mind.

There is no one thing that makes you happy, but the one thing that can control the happiness in your life is you.   It is your attitude and understanding of happiness that sets the bar.   We should not set the bar so high that too much is required in reaching it. Sometimes, we have desires and wants that we believe will bring us happiness, but when they don't, we begin looking for something else.   Before searching around the world for that happiness, look first in the mirror and in your own backyard.

First thing in the morning, tell yourself it is going to be a great day.   Thank God for your job, your family, your friends, your health, your knowledge and ask for wisdom.   Life and its components create happiness   It is how you (yes you) choose to live it.

HE WHO KNEELS BEFORE GOD CAN STAND BEFORE ANYTHING.

This act of kneeling, without a believing faith, will give you nothing more than sore knees. It's the faith that will give you the power that is within God's promises, the power of prayer, hope, wisdom, and courage. "...All things are possible to him that believeth" (Mark 9:23). This is power to stand before any adversity.

To kneel before a most powerful God is just a gesture; what He needs to see is the faith that is within you. However, anytime we take the action of kneeling before God (to show our humility or reverence) it reveals our faith and trust. When we use this gesture, it must communicate what is within our heart. Kneeling before God helps maintain a humble attitude, putting in perspective our relationship with God: our father, creator, and protector. Kneeling before God allows us to open our heart, pouring out our soul, spilling it at the feet of God, keeping ourselves humble. In consideration of these thoughts, I believe kneeling is pleasing to God (Psalms 24:4-5).

Who do we have to stand before? The devil is our greatest threat. Standing against the devil, upholding our Christian beliefs to the world is our challenge. The devil controls daily temptations: those things of a worldly or devilish notion that tempt us to relax our faith in God. Anytime we relax our faith in God, it is pleasing to the devil.

As believers we know our prayers will be heard, and our battles will be fought with God by our side. God does not fight the battles for us, but He gives us the strength and wisdom to fight until victory is achieved. Romans 8:31 "...If God is for us, who can be against us?"

We need to kneel, whether we choose to go to our knees or not. We need to "kneel" our lives: humbling ourselves before God. How can this act of humility be so powerful? Because this humble action is a believing action and with adoration we honor Him as Father of all creation, and we know that everything is possible for him who believes (Mark 9:25).

"I LOVE YOU.
BE MINE."
JESUS CHRIST.
(Valentine's Day)

"No one has greater love than to lay down his life for another" (John 15:13). This was Jesus' biggest "I Love You." All He asks in return... we love Him.

How do we return such love? How can we measure this love to balance the scales? The fact is we cannot. We can only try to realize the magnitude of His love and reciprocate within our abilities. God has given us these abilities; by studying the Word, we can learn to embrace love as our hope for humanity. By showing this love, we will let the light of Christ shine for the world to see.

Love is always around us. Love is mentioned 505 times in the N.I.V. Bible and 280 times in the King James. Sometimes we have to seek his love, and sometimes we only need to recognize it. God tells us He loves us and we are told to love Him. When Jesus was asked to reveal the greatest commandment, he responded, "Love the Lord your God with all your heart and with all your soul and with all your mind and with all your strength. The second is this: Love your neighbor as yourself. There is no commandment greater than these" (Mark 12:30-32).

We express love to God by studying the teachings of Christ and setting our goals to be of a sinless nature. We can begin this expression of love with small baby steps. In fact, it should start when we are children. We should teach our children to love humanity, take away hate, and take away all prejudices.

What does love do for us? God has promised that in all things He works for the good of those who love Him (Romans 8:28). Love is to be given and love is to be received. My car license tag ends with the letters "LDM" and in order to recall this I have remembered the expression "Love Does Much." For example...

- Love is nurturing as a child.
- Love is encouragement when we are down.
- Love is a simple gesture of courtesy on a stressful day.
- Love is someone listening when we are troubled.
- Love is a birthday wish from a friend.
- Love is an unexpected visit from a friend.
- Love is breakfast prepared for us in the morning.

- Love is a warm smile when we have done something good.
- Love is a weapon over hate.
- Cherish love for what it is. It is the new law: salvation established through Christ.

Love is many things that we take for granted. You can feel it in a hug or a smile. Love is not always spoken, but you know it's there. Learn to recognize love. It is needed to experience life to its fullest.

I believe there is more love in the world than hate. Prove me right!

IF GOD IS
YOUR CO-PILOT,
YOU BETTER
SWITCH SEATS.

If a pilot in training gets in trouble, the flight instructor will quickly take over the controls. The proper method in transferring this piloting of the plane is the pilot in training announces to the flight instructor he is transferring the controls. The flight instructor, in turn, affirms the request by stating he has control of the plane. I have a total of 6 hours actual flying time as a student pilot. I am one of the few people who can get four touchdowns on a single landing. In times like these, I need that flight instructor.

God is like the flight instructor; He can step in and take control. He is more able than I to pilot my life. The controls are within me, but the know-how is within God. If we are trying to pilot our lives without God, we will make numerous near fatal mistakes. Our life is guided by the knowledge we receive. If we believe through knowledge and ask for help (repent and be baptized), we will receive it.

John 14:14 "You may ask me for anything in my name, and I will do it."

There is a song that, in fact, has won numerous awards entitled, *Jesus Take the Wheel*, which reiterates this thought. It tells of the struggle of a young woman and her child when she is near the end of her rope. When life gets you down, you will need a pilot, someone to take the wheel of your life. Many times life just takes a turn for the worst. There is no one to blame, in particular, because it is no one's fault. Even if there is a cause and effect, the main point is to pick up the pieces and hand them to God. With His direction, being the experienced pilot he is, you will pull out of the tailspin or the crash course and recover from the stall.

I believe God is always sitting in the pilot's seat of life. But, like the flight instructor, you have to ask him to take the controls. We do this by accepting Christ as our savior and understanding that he died for our sins. This is the announcement you must make for God to take over control. Your free will to reject the devil is just the command God is waiting for. You announce to God, your flight instructor, that you are ready. Your announcement to God can be made by simply acknowledging that you have failed without Him and want to learn to fly using his manual as your flight manual. Work with a believing church to secure your knowledge. By fulfilling his commands, you can have God piloting your life.

IF YOU WANT YOUR WORDS TO CARRY WEIGHT... MEASURE THEM CAREFULLY.

Words fail me, at least those words that express my feelings or desires to another person. I have difficulty in this area. But, it seems that words are not the issue. The issue is the understanding in which I present those words and the understanding in which they are received. Communication is a two way street. What you say is in one lane and is met by what is heard. There are many books on the subject that primarily deal with the business aspect of how to say things or ask things in order to get a favorable response. However, when it comes to issues of everyday life, communications seem not to have a defined goal. Why could we not apply some of the same theories to everyday life? We don't carefully analyze how our words will be received - our meanings may be different. I'm not sure this will ever be resolved. Things will always be misunderstood.

I once said to a supervisor that the goals of the company were overwhelming. The next thing I knew he pulled me aside and suggested that I take a leave of absence. He took me for my word. But, all I meant to say was the goals were beyond reason for the time frame allotted - not that it was emotionally draining and I was at a point of a nervous breakdown.

Should we, in caution, classify people and communicate appropriately by choosing different words for each classification - using one set of words for left brain thinkers and yet another set of words for right brain thinkers? Or, choose words for those who are positive thinkers differently than for negative thinkers? Where should we stop? People come from many varied backgrounds which will create many different classifications.

Rhonda and I have always known that communication in our business was very important. We wanted our communication to our customers and to our employees to be understood in the same manner that it was intended. We found this to be very difficult. We even made a slogan to help in this area. In 1988, we made a resolution to "Communicate in 88." This helped us become aware of communication. But, how much we advanced in communication was not determined. It is still an issue of individual understanding.

If I have learned one thing in communicating: there is no one thing. It is not universal. What is heard is rooted in the mind of the one that is listening and what is said is rooted in the mind of the one that is talking. To put these two actions in unison is a rarity. Possibly, this is when friendships or companionships are formed.

However, there are words that are clearly understood. We should avoid such words as stupid, dumb, and other slang and degrading words. These words have a universal hurt when directed at another individual and a negative effect on any conversation. It would be very difficult for a conversation or action to end in a unified, win-win situation when these words are used.

You have heard it said it only takes one second to form a first impression. Well, it only takes one word to remove all doubt about this impression. Our character is revealed by the words we use. Our desires are revealed by words. We need to make sure that our words are saying what we intend them to mean. This is where I have fallen short. But I continue to seek insight and understanding.

I am very envious of those who are smooth communicators. They somehow develop choices in words: assembling them to display an understanding, and at the same time, remove all rough edges. These people seem to advance in society and become admired leaders. They seem to get things done... with full cooperation from their team.

For those of us who realize this, and continue to seek wisdom, there is hope. Hope in knowing that if we are seeking wisdom, it can be found. Our efforts will be rewarded through seeking.

What am I talking about here? Some would say that I am referring to seeking Christ, the hope of salvation. Others would say that I am referring to the knowledge of communicating. Both would be correct. Finding words within a heart dedicated to Christ will be the hope needed to find the right words.

Sometimes it takes many words to express your true feelings, if so, use many words. Fewer words sometime leave the wrong impression.

Communicate and initiate your words cautiously, but yet deliberately, with humility and gentility, as if you held the heart of a teacher, brother, sister, mother, father, lover or friend.

IN SPITE OF THE HIGH COST OF LIVING, IT IS STILL POPULAR.

We all enjoy life. We don't want to die. Some of us don't fear dying, but we don't want to do anything to encourage it either. I would like to address living, not the opposite of dying, but about how we live, the whole of living, and what we do with our life. The cost mentioned in the marquee saying is not about money, but about time, effort and, in essence, what we do with our lives. If it is wasted, then our living is sub-par. If we use time to better ourselves, in all areas, then living becomes rewarding.

If asked, we all say we are living. Just because we are walking, talking and breathing, are we, in fact, living? I believe we are living only when we are utilizing a minimum of seventy-five percent of our capabilities. Some are merely surviving, doing only what it takes. Living is an attitude about life itself, being happy to have a job, being happy to have a family, being happy to have a home. Living should be synonymous with happy.

Enjoying all the blessings God has given and continues to give us would insure happiness.

Living is more than breathing, it is being alive. Alive is being excited about the things we do daily, enthusiastic and thankful about being all that we can be. We must be thankful for everything: our health- no matter how bad it is or how bad we feel, there is always someone who is worse than we are; our job- think of those who do not have one, who truly want one; our home – no matter if we feel it is too small, there are those without one. Living is being happy with what we have and seeking our full potential.

The high cost of living is dying. If we are not alive, we are dead. Remember, it is how we lived that will determine how we live (our eternal life).

Having a loving attitude, increasing our knowledge (growing intellectually and spiritually), valuing what we have, creating a foundation and following God's plan for eternal salvation is "living."

IN TRYING TIMES…
DON'T QUIT TRYING.

I have heard it said "when the going gets tough, the tough get going." This attitude is what it takes to strive in trying times. We simply dig a little harder when the ground gets harder. If we don't, then we don't get the job accomplished. Anything worth doing is worth completing, regardless of how difficult it may be.

Doing something that improves our health, finances, and/or relationships in a positive way can be a catalyst that leads to correcting or improving problems in these areas. We must not quit. We may change our priorities, but we must never quit. Quitting is loosing hope, and we will never loose hope. We may misplace it, but it will always be there when we seek it.

Sometimes we quit too soon because we don't have a plan, and we get overwhelmed with these difficulties. That's what trying times are ….difficulties in life. I would suggest making a "plan of attack" to help put these difficulties in perspective. Take a sheet of paper and write down these difficulties that are challenging your life in a column on the left and in a column on the right list how you can improve or erase this particular difficulty. This technique systematically approaches the problem, rather than approaching it with an emotional reaction: which usually does not solve the problem, it just creates worry and anxiety. I believe you can take charge of personal items, family situations and business difficulties with this technique. This technique forces you to acknowledge that you have a problem and provides a method for a solution.

Example

Problem	Solution
Not enough money at the end of the month.	Make a budget to find out where the money is going.
I am late for work and my boss is getting angry.	Duh! Set the alarm earlier and plan to be at work ahead of schedule.
My wife is angry because I spend too much time with the guys.	Duh! Here is where you set priorities in your life. Make sure your family is right up there.
My family history shows heart problems.	Plan to eat right, exercise and avoid stress

I don't mean to oversimplify this. It takes enormous effort just to admit or face difficulties and this plan gets you started in the right direction.   It is a choice you must make if you want to be in charge of your own life.   Not doing this allows the devil to win.

You must have hope.   Hope gives you the motivation and energies to persevere.   Many times it is less difficult to succumb to defeat (to give up) allowing depression, anger and addiction to invade your life.   This is when you should take a lesson from the tough.   Learn this toughness and take control of your life.

The sooner we approach trying situations, the sooner we can do something about them.   It is your choice.   There are many situations in life we blame on family history (our hereditary traits), but I don't believe this should be the scapegoat.   We are individual creatures, created in the likeness of God and our lives are the result of the choices we make. Don't quit...persevere.

IT IS BETTER TO LOOK AHEAD AND PLAN THAN TO LOOK BACK AND REGRET.

Today is the first day of the rest of your life. What we do today determines what happens tomorrow. What happened yesterday is lost forever. We can only change now forward.

Do any of these short, but pungent, remarks hit you? It is all about planning for tomorrow and taking action today. The desires that make up our wish list must move into a plan of action today before they can be realized. When I refer to a wish list, I am not referring to the one you make at Christmas time-as gifts to receive. I am referring to anything you have desired, whether it is a position in life, spiritual fulfillment, an achievement of learning, or something of a smaller nature. Anything that has been a gnawing desire within your subconscious should be on this list. First, I would recommend prioritizing the list: most desired to least desired. I believe that once you achieve the most important thing on your list, you will get so much gratification you will move to the next with lightning speed.

There is nothing more gratifying than to take an old worry and eliminate it. An old worry (something that is weighting on your mind) clogs our abilities and reduces our peace, joy and happiness.

As time goes by, these undone things on your list become regrets. It is said that we have more regrets of things we failed to do than of things we have done. Completing top priority things on our list would eliminate these regrets. If your list is too long and it overwhelms you, take a close look and eliminate those things that surpass your current capabilities. Work first on the things that can be accomplished with current capabilities. You will find that as things are accomplished, you will gain the momentum necessary to finish, even going back and tackling those most difficult ones that you passed over.

The forward focus of this topic is my answer to obtaining the motivation needed to begin working on your wish list. Forward-thinking is the same as hope. We cannot hope to change the past. Hope comes from the ability to direct the future by the actions taken today.

It is necessary to tell yourself that things are good - only if I make them good. We control our destiny. I just keep using these short, one-liners, but they are so true. The future is only what we make it. Oh, my goodness, another one. Life is too short to leave out a little humor.

To end my thoughts on this message, I will refer you to all the other messages that say it is all up to you and the action you take today.

The greatest plan for tomorrow is the "plan" Christ places before us today; accept this plan and have no regrets.

IT IS EASIER TO
TELL THE TRUTH
THAN HIDE IT.

The lie begins without the truth. Why? Why do we find it necessary to lie? Here are some reasons...

- We fear the truth.
- We don't want to be wrong.
- We don't want to apologize.
- We need to be right.
- We want others to be wrong.
- We want something we don't deserve.

God tells us not to lie in one of his commandments (Exodus 20:16). Lying not only deceives others, but deceives our self-image as well. Those who are not comfortable with themselves tend to lie, thinking it is easier to lie than "take action" to correct or improve themselves to the point where they would not have to lie. They choose to lie because their self-image is too low to fight the fear. Improving your self-image and self-confidence would result in not having the need or desire to tell a lie. It takes a stronger person to tell the truth. Strength is in the truth.

I have always advocated telling the truth. Not only because it is the right thing to do, but because it causes less pain than lying. In my retail business, I emphasized admitting fault to customers rather than covering up. The customer's trust is more valuable than my pride. The reward, of course, was developing friends and repeat customers. I cannot remember ever wishing I had lied.

If we always tell the truth, we don't get caught in a lie. We should not be afraid of the truth, but afraid of the lie. Lying is more difficult to do than telling the truth: "If you tell the truth, you don't have to remember anything."- Mark Twain.

Lying can be difficult and it creates pain. Pain comes when you get caught in a lie: loosing something or someone you love because no one can trust you. Most of the time, lying is like an addiction, one doesn't know when to stop. Old lies breed new lies; therefore, you become known as a liar: "Repetition does not transform a lie" - Franklin Roosevelt.

One of the best ways to increase your self-esteem is to always tell the truth and not hide from it. This makes you feel good about yourself. Truth also improves the way others think of you. Your ideas and thoughts mean more to others and you will grow your self-confidence. We need others in our lives and this can only happen if we are truthful: "If you continue in my work, then you are my disciples...And you shall know the truth, and the truth shall make you free" (John 8:32).

We should all tell the truth as it is known.

IF THERE IS SWEETNESS
IN REVENGE,
THERE IS BITTERNESS
IN THE HEART.

TRIUMPH
IS JUST
UMPH ADDED
TO TRY.

THE MAGNIFICENT OAK TREE
WAS ONCE
A LITTLE NUT
THAT HELD ITS GROUND.

JUST LIKE BUTTER,
A RUMOR IS HARD
TO UNSPREAD.

A SMILE
ADDS TO YOUR FACE VALUE.

IT IS GOOD TO BE A CHRISTIAN AND KNOW IT. IT IS BETTER TO BE A CHRISTIAN AND SHOW IT.

What should we display to show we are Christians? Do we need to wear a cross around our neck? Do we stand on a street corner and wave the Bible? Should one praise God with every breath? All of these things could indicate Christian faith. Some of these things could appear to be religious exploits or just a fashion statement and not an indication of proclaiming faith.

I am a member of the Church of Christ, and we are conservative in nature. But, it doesn't take much to be labeled a hypocrite. Just a simple un-Christian like act would turn on critics, turn off the non-practicing Christian and make it difficult to encourage the non-Christian. This makes me wonder: will I be labeled a hypocrite if I display this proclamation of faith, and then am caught doing something un-Christian like? Will this create ambiguity and justify someone's decision in not becoming a Christian? Don't get me wrong, I want to display my faith. I want to justify my faith. But, we are all imperfect people, and life will step in and make it difficult to display a Christ-like image. We must keep focused, overcoming these moments, and building our "faith-esteem."

I want to display my belief with something obvious without being tagged a weirdo. I would wear a nametag with "I am a Christian" engraved on it, but I would be persecuted, labeled as the one with the nametag, or "holier than thou," among a number of other expletives. Possibly, something more subtle: a small pin or a cross, but then I might be labeled a groupie and not necessarily make evident my personal relationship with God. What is left? Even a pagan can be honest, ethical, well dressed, a good neighbor, good father, charitable or anything else that one of Christian faith should be or do. What ... what?

I think we need to do good things. We need to say good things. We set priorities in our life that say "no" to questionable activities. We train our children to do the same. We do this to glorify Jesus and proclaim his way as our way. We talk to people at work with no reluctance in mentioning our faith and where we go to church. I don't mean for this to be the first thing we say when we meet someone, just when it is appropriate in conversation. Tell people the positive things Christ has done in your life. I bring this up because I have recently heard a story about the death of a man in which fellow co-workers did not even know the deceased was a Christian, some of whom had been co-workers for a number of years. Be proud of your faith and not ashamed. If you are ashamed of your faith, then carefully examine your faith and determine if it is your faith or the people of your particular "faith circle" that you are ashamed; possibly they don't justify your faith.

We should live our lives with Christ in our heart. To those with whom we come in contact (friends we see often, strangers we meet for the first time, people who serve us in restaurants, who deliver our mail, or service our automobiles), we can display our faith in Christ through our actions. Being Christ-like is an enormous responsibility, and we will err on occasion, but our heart needs to maintain love for our fellow earthlings and love for our Heavenly Father. James 2:18 "But someone will say, 'You have faith; I have deeds.' Show me your faith without deeds, and I will show you my faith by what I do."

With the love and sprit of God, our faith should be displayed in our eyes, our smiling face, our helping hands, and should roll off our tongue and through our lips.

JUSTIFYING
YOUR FAULT...
DOUBLES IT.

I will say first: we all have faults. Something was said by our preacher during a sermon that has stuck with me. He said that we are all imperfect people. This made an impression on me, not so much that we are an inferior group of people, but, that we all have something in common. Anyone who enters the assembly is imperfect. I can look to the person to the right of me and then look to the left and then look in the mirror and know that we share this characteristic of imperfection. We, of course, know we should constantly try to improve, but, as much as we try, we cannot be perfect. But, rather than admit our faults, we try to cover them up by justifying them.

One of the greatest challenges we face in life is learning how to deal with mistakes. I have known for a long time that it is by making mistakes that we learn. We hear of the achievements of the rich, famous and powerful. They tell us of their difficulties and how much they learned from their mistakes. Yet, it is still hard for me to disregard the unpleasantness of making a mistake. I am not reaching my full potential because I fear the pain of making a mistake. I know that I learn and grow from my mistakes; it is my responsibility to change and prevent the same mistake from happening again.

We double our faults by blaming others, failing to own up to our mistakes, and denying they ever happened. The mistakes we make in life are our responsibility. The responsible thing to do is admit the things that are our fault. It is easy to see how one mistake leads to another creating a snowball effect - with faults piling up, thereby, damaging our character.

Justifying your faults clogs your pipes. By this, I mean justifying your faults creates a breakdown in your stream of mental thoughts, disrupting positive, more constructive thoughts and clogging moral and ethical decision making capabilities. Admit your faults so you don't create new faults building onto old ones. You want to keep your mental and emotional pipes clean.

Once clogged, we need a pipe cleaner - we then can start anew. Christ is that pipe cleaner. We can bring our faults to him and he will forgive and erase; we can then start a new life with a new direction, with clean mental and emotional pipes.

KIND WORDS
ARE ALWAYS
THE RIGHT WORDS.

Sticks and stones break bones, but words hurt too. We can be cruel sometimes with our words. It once was said that we put our mouth in motion before putting our brain in gear. Our words are powerful. They can change the course of a nation. The words of our president can pull a nation together as those words did after the great depression. Words are used by counselors to put lives back together. Those are all good words. But words can also hurt and tear down a person's self-image and set a future of doubt.

As young people, we are molded by words and example. We are limited at a young age as to who sets those examples. But, at an older age we have choices. Do not choose to be around those who use unkind words on a regular basis.

Unkind words or name calling are detrimental to building the proper self-image. For example, avoid using these words: stupid, idiot, or fool.

Kind words, however, show praise and love. For example, use these words: good job, you can do it, and I'm sorry. These are words that build up one's self-image.

Words that encourage us to do better are kind words. Unkind words usually come from the dark side. By the dark side, I mean from hate or anger, neither of which can serve good.

Remember, it is better to say nothing than to use unkind words. If you have nothing good to say, then say nothing. We must analyze (think) before we speak. Anger has the tendency to bring forth unkind words. We must talk to ourselves, asking if this is the right time to discuss the matter, or should we wait until we have cooled down: selecting a time when we can choose the words with more controlled thought. Remember, words are to be used productively, not destructively.

Disappointment tempts us to use unkind words. Say that you're disappointed, rather than use words that are most often regretted. There is no rewind button in life. It is hard to take back words that have already been spoken.

Sometimes words mean different things to different people. Be careful with individual words, sometimes it takes complex sentences to fully express your feelings.

Express words that show love for mankind, that represent good, not evil. The dictionary is full of words...choose wisely.

HOW DO YOU GET TO HEAVEN
FROM (YOUR TOWN)?
APPLY WITHIN.

IF GOD SEEMS SO FAR AWAY...
GUESS WHO MOVED.

IF YOU HAVE A BAD TEMPER...
DON'T LOOSE IT.

IF YOUR BIBLE IS FALLING APART,
CHANCES ARE YOUR LIFE IS STAYING
TOGETHER.

IT IS BETTER TO LOOK AHEAD AND PLAN THAN
TO LOOK BACK AND REGRET.

IT TAKES BOTH RAIN AND SUNSHINE
TO MAKE A RAINBOW.

LAUGHTER IS THE SUNSHINE
THAT MELTS THE WINTER OFF YOUR FACE.

LIFE ON EARTH
IS A DRESS REHEARSAL FOR ETERNITY.

MAKE THE
BEST OF IT
WHEN YOU GET
THE WORST OF IT.

"Life is like a box of chocolates, you never know what you're going to get." This is my favorite quote from the movie *Forest Gump*. It is not so much what we get, but how we deal with it that matters. If we are given a lemon, make lemonade.

Life should be enjoyable. Our expectations of life should be such. It may seem that some handle their burdens and trials better than others. This may be so, but not because they are smarter or stronger. The reason is that they have made the decision to respond rather than do nothing. The requirements to achieve this joyful life are hope and action. The action is the most important; it turns the hope into reality. Those who know what needs to be done and do nothing are foolish. Those who take action are powerful and can direct their own lives.

Sometimes dealing with our trials requires help, which is a sign of strength through determination. Accepting help would be considered an acceptable action. Taking action, whether by accepting or asking for help or by tackling the problem ourselves, will be required to accomplish the best results of a bad situation. We should allow those who are close to us to help: family, close friends and professionals. It is not necessary to deal with every situation by ourselves; however, it is our responsibility. Above all, we should ask God to help.

Sometimes we ask God for help and it seems that we don't see results. I feel that there are always results. God answers prayers as yes, no or later. I think that even though we don't immediately see results, changes happen in our life that, in essence, creates an opportunity for us to answer the prayer. A change is an answered prayer. Change is necessary to improve any bad situation. After all, if we keep doing what we are doing, we keep getting what we are getting. If things are not improving with life as it is happening, change must take place. In order to effect a change in our life, something has to test our comfort zone (a routine lifestyle that we are comfortable with). Having the ability to relinquish the comfort zone is something that all successful people have. It is something that we all must do at sometime in our life. It is usually in "have to" cases. I think of it as doing what has to be done to correct a particular situation in a positive manner (take action).

James 1:1-8 "James, a servant of God and of the Lord Jesus Christ, To the twelve tribes scattered among the nations: Greetings. Consider it pure joy, my brothers, whenever you face trials of many kinds, because you know that the testing of your faith develops perseverance. Perseverance must finish its work so that you may be mature and complete, not lacking anything. If any of you lacks wisdom, he should ask God, who gives generously to all without finding fault, and it will be given to him. But when he asks, he must believe and not doubt, because he who doubts is like a wave of the sea, blown and tossed by the wind. That man should not think he will receive anything from the Lord; he is a double-minded man, unstable in all he does."

Have you considered that God may want to change you? Words are written by those who would like to make an impact on your life. These words are read and hopefully trigger emotions or thoughts, and you decide either to take action or to do nothing.

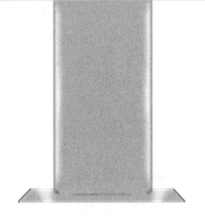

MORE PEOPLE FAIL FROM LACK OF PURPOSE THAN LACK OF TALENT.

One of my favorite storytellers is Paul Harvey. I recently heard him tell the story of an individual, somewhat a recluse, who would sit in his room with windows and doors closed, writing short stories. He was gaining no pleasure or happiness from his life until a forced meeting led him to the love of his life. He found his first love, and from that moment on, he had purpose in his life. Of course, "the rest of the story" is that this late bloomer was Nathaniel Hawthorne, possibly best known for great literary works, such as, *The Scarlet Letter* and *The House of Seven Gables*.

Our purpose in life is the driving force behind our talent. All of us have talents, but the success of those talents is to find a purpose to use them. In the case of Hawthorne, he had written short stories; but they failed to sustain his creativity. Once an event such as love for another fueled his talents, great works appeared.

If you were to employ a "talent coach" to improve your talents, what talent would they improve? If you don't know what your talents are, just ask your best friend. Once the friend reveals their opinion, spend time in meditation to see if you can agree. I would also recommend searching "within" for your talents. Your talents can be revealed through an inward search, fueled by the desire to locate these talents. The desire would be created by the realization or understanding of these God given talents. Ask God, through prayer, what you can do with this talent. Our talents, if properly utilized, could either develop into a career that would substantially change your life or they could be talents that could substantially change someone else's life. In fact, they could change a multitude of people's lives. I am speaking, of course, changing in a good way.

The "purpose" is a vision of fulfillment; a vision that is channeled through spiritual and intellectual filters, utilizing your talents, with the "purpose" fueling your efforts. With this statement, it is my intent to emphasize that a goal set without consulting the word of God, would not be a worthwhile goal. Therefore, a purpose without the same would not be a worthwhile purpose.

We are full of talents; some are not obvious to us. Some are slightly hidden and we have been afraid of letting them out. Don't deprive the world of these talents; let them be known. Sure, they may have to be improved, but don't go through life without celebrating your talents. What if Abe Lincoln had quit after his first defeat? What if David had never thrown that first stone? How would history have been changed? Personally, what if I had never written my first page? A wonderful experience would not have been realized.

**THE BEST PREPARATION FOR TOMORROW
IS LIVING WELL TODAY.**

**THE BEST THING TO SAVE
FOR THE FUTURE
IS YOUR SOUL.**

**THE GREATEST FAULT
IS BELIEVING YOU HAVE NONE.**

**THE GREATEST GIFT YOU CAN GIVE SOMEONE
IS YOUR TIME.**

**THE GREATEST OXYMORON...
LIVING IN SIN.**

**THE ONE WHO IS WORST THAT THE QUITTER IS
THE ONE WHO NEVER BEGINS.**

THINK TWICE BEFORE SAYING NOTHING.

NEVER ENTER THE ARENA EXPECTING TO LOSE.

I remember watching Charles Stanley on TV. It was New Years Day and I was away from home. The topic was "Our Exceptional Lives." It was part of a series, and I only heard one segment. Today's topic was expecting to win, expecting what God has promised us. How appropriate for this message. Many times I have been inspired to write on specific topics from events that happen in the present or maybe events happen because I am beginning to write on specific topics. I believe either is possible.

So many times we start the day with negative thoughts. Why do we do this? Being optimistic is not a sin; in fact, it is said that what the righteous desire will be granted (Proverbs 10:24). I quote the following often, "If you think you can or you think you can't, you're right." One of my favorite motivational trainers, Zig Ziglar, uses this quote. Others have said many similar statements including James Allen, in his book *As a Man Thinketh So Is He*, in which he credits Proverbs 23:7. I believe the outcome of any situation is determined greatly by the attitude you have going into the situation. Winners enter the arena expecting to win.

Let's look at the story of David and Goliath. When this small shepherd boy approached the giant, he approached with confidence, a confidence that had been proven time and again. His faith told him that God was with him. He had made the proper preparation through his previous battles protecting the sheep from bears and lions. This had given him the experience and skills needed to build this confidence. He entered the arena expecting to win. This story is told in 1 Samuel 17:34-49.

If you expect to win, you are more apt to prepare yourself. Spending more time in preparation will greatly improve your performance. We witness this everyday by those who are winners. Winners are not just those in competitive sports. Winners are those who achieve their goals. They loose weight, build strength, quit smoking, make the deal, read a book, or complete a project. What makes them winners? They go into the arena expecting to win. They make the necessary preparation to win. They set priorities that lead them in the direction of winning.

I have heard it said, "They just have determination and motivation that I don't have." It is not something that some people have and others do not. It is something that anyone can have. It is a choice, a mental decision to do what is necessary. The fact is that you are capable of developing determination. Your talents lie within you. Your knowledge can be increased, your body can be strengthened, and you can improve your life with this simple realization.

God wants positive people— people who are sure of their belief and prepare for their future by studying and learning more about achieving the goals set by Christ.

It is what you say to yourself that can change a negative outlook into a positive outlook.

Tell yourself "I CAN!"

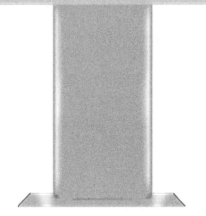

NEVER GIVE THE DEVIL A RIDE. HE WILL WANT TO DRIVE.

I would never give the devil a ride. Who would give a guy, in a red suit with horns and a long tail, a ride? Is this the picture you see when the devil is mentioned? I don't think this is actually what the devil looks like. If someone should ask me to draw the devil, I would admit, I would probably draw such a character. It would be wonderful if he were that easy to recognize. But, the truth is, he wears many disguises, and he is not a character - he is real.

The devil's joy is tempting people to sin. He chooses to disguise himself with temptations that are not obviously clothed as sin. We are never forced into sin. Temptations allow us the opportunity to make choices. Sin does not have a big red "S" with blazes, so these temptations can be deceitful. Whether on television or words in a song, we are tempted and influenced by those in the media. We can make a choice to avoid these things, and we can also choose the people and places we allow to influence us.

Possibly the best way to avoid sin is to focus on God. The devil is the spirit of evil, while God is the spirit of good. If we focus on good, it will make evil the adversary. It would be better to be on the side of good. I believe good will win out over evil.

I don't think we want to sin. We yield to sin because it is disguised as pleasure. Once sin is experienced as pleasure, it becomes more and more difficult to avoid. In fact, we find ourselves searching for greater sin disguised as greater pleasure. This is when the devil is driving.

God is the one who should be driving. I want "good" behind the wheel, not evil. In the war, good verses evil, I want to be on the side of good. The rewards are greater. I'll choose streets paved with gold over fire and brimstone any day.

OFTEN ATTITUDE IS THE ONLY DIFFERENCE BETWEEN SUCCESS AND FAILURE.

Attitude Is Everything, a book written by Keith Harrell, rejuvenated my thinking about how attitude is so important in our lives.　Our attitude about anything and everything controls our thoughts and actions, exposing our character to the world. William James, a great twentieth-century psychologist, once said, "The greatest discovery of my generation is that a human being can alter his life by altering his attitudes of mind."　Simply put, if you want to change, change your attitude.

There are many reasons we have the attitude we have, but let's just concentrate on where our attitude has gotten us, and where it is taking us.　So ask yourself, "Am I happy with my life today?"　If your answer is "No," then you may need an attitude adjustment.　How do we get an attitude adjustment? It is not something that you can order from the local chiropractor or health spa.　It comes through trials and efforts.　You can do as I have done: read books on the subject, listen to talks and do other research.

You will find just about every self-help book ever written will list attitude as the determining factor between failure and success. Growing through knowledge can help us improve our attitude, but it can be an arduous task. It requires determination, responsibility, enthusiasm, ambition, and motivation (DREAM).

We all should want to have the attitude of Jesus. The beatitudes, as we call them, are examples Christ gave during the Sermon on the Mount. They are great to help us establish some of the core characteristics of our attitude.

Attitude of Spirituality...
Mathew 5:3 "Blessed are the poor in spirit: for theirs is the kingdom of heaven." Poor as mentioned here, means full.

A Loving Attitude...
Mathew 5:4 "Blessed are they that mourn: for they shall be comforted."

Attitude of Gentleness through Humility.
Mathew 5:5 "Blessed are the meek: for they shall inherit the earth."

Morality and integrity
Mathew 5:6 "Blessed are they which do hunger and thirst after righteousness: for they shall be filled."

Compassionate Attitude
Mathew 5:7 "Blessed are the merciful: for they shall obtain mercy."

Balance Mind, Heart and Will with all Attitudes...
Mathew 5:8 "Blessed are the pure in heart: for they shall see God."

Attitude of Forgiveness
Mathew 5:9 "Blessed are the peacemakers: for they shall be called the children of God."

Enduring Attitude
Mathew 5:10 "Blessed are they which are persecuted for righteousness' sake: for theirs is the kingdom of heaven."

Attitude of Resolve
Mathew 5:11 "Blessed are ye, when men shall revile you, and persecute you, and shall say all manner of evil against you falsely, for my sake."

In the book *Lead Like Jesus,* written by Dr. Kenneth Blanchard and Phil Hodges, the most important attitude is equal to that of a servant: being focused as Jesus was focused.

Have an attitude of a servant leader, not of a self-servant leader.

PLAN AHEAD...
NOAH DIDN'T
BUILD THE ARK
IN THE RAIN.

The main point of this marquee is to emphasize planning: making preparations today for what will be needed tomorrow. It is important to live today, but part of living today must be planning for tomorrow. We must plan for that rainy day (pun intended). We must plan our future based on what we know today. So I encourage you to make a list of things you will need in the future and include in that list the way you will fulfill those needs. You must keep in consideration that Murphy may pay a visit, so prepare for an emergency. It is important to know what our needs will be today and in the future. We should not waste time and money today, leaving ourselves in need later in life. Work with what you have today, and make plans for tomorrow, but don't use tomorrow's resources to live on today. It is a must to plan for growth, but you will have to do what is necessary today to fulfill that plan. In other words, make the plan and take action on the plan.

I can remember growing up on a farm and heating our home with a wood burning stove. We knew that winter would come and we would need wood to burn for heat. We knew approximately how much we would need based on the amount we used the previous year. I can remember an extremely bad winter in which we ran short. We moved in with my grandfather in order to consolidate our firewood supply to make it last the season. Even after we did this, we had to cut more firewood. If you have ever tried to cut and split frozen wood, you know what difficulty we had. Sometimes even the best plans do not meet the needs of the unexpected. But, any plan is better than no plan at all.

According to Brian Headd in a report from the US Small Business Administration, 50% of businesses close four years after starting. The majority of these did not have a business plan.

Any successful entrepreneur will tell you that you need a business plan before you open a new business or purchase an ongoing business. Noah was given a plan, and he followed that plan. The job was completed as planned.

Planning can sometimes seem to be a waste of time, but it is quite the opposite. When Noah was given the job of building the ark, he knew how much material was needed and how long it would take because God gave him the plan. Noah did as he had been asked, and at the appropriate time, it began to rain for forty days and forty nights just as God had said. If Noah had not followed the plan, we wouldn't be here today.

We need to put things in our plan that build relationships, as well a house, things that restore faith as well as an antique car, and things that support our church as well as our profession. Our plan for salvation is recorded in the Bible; we need to make sure we take action on this plan: the greatest plan of all.

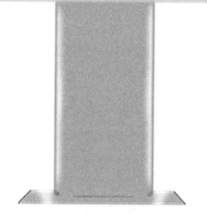

SMILES
ARE LIKE
ECHOES.

You are not fully dressed without a smile; if you are happy, tell your face; a smile uses fewer muscles than a frown. These truisms were created to show the importance of a smile. The reasons are overwhelmingly supportive: initiating a desired personality trait, improving communication skills, and developing influential success and friendship building characteristics. The smile is the outer expression of the soul. The reason it is like echoes is because most smiles are reciprocated.

I just saw a small portion of the TV show *Extreme Makeover* when they were visiting New Orleans after hurricane Katrina. Many homes and contents were almost completely destroyed by the flood and wind. The residents were devastated that their family photos were practically unrecognizable. The person (all I remember is Pat) contacted the star of the show (Ty) to see if anything could be done to restore these photos. He contacted HP, the computer and printer people, to see if they could help. They sent a portable photo lab to the area and restored these photos. The smiles I saw from the people who received these restored photos were very memorable. They were smiles of gratitude, smiles of love, and smiles of hope that echoed all the way to me and to millions of others who saw this program.

Smiles communicate our inward expressions to others. Smiles are like a gift: something given without anticipations. Smiles will express our desire to communicate favorably, our compassion, sympathy, hope, wisdom, knowledge, and faith.

A smile is part of that first impression we give to others. That impression containing a smile is of one who is happy with life, enjoying the day, and pleased to be in your presence. A smile makes one enjoyable to be around, setting the attitude of a conversation. With a smile, you can give hope and receive hope. It is a universal language: the smile can be understood in any language.

I have to practice smiling often. It is not as natural for me as I would like it to be. For many years I have been telling myself that I prefer to smile. I smile within, but it is the aesthetic part that I have to practice, you know, actually bringing the corners of my lips upward and showing my teeth. If you are happy, tell your face, I have to tell my face.

For many, the smile comes naturally, but for many, like me, it takes practice to develop. The subconscious will learn to do this, but you must teach it. You must first decide that smiling is for you. Then you must convince your conscious mind to begin the training process. The way to begin your teaching is by talking to yourself. Talking to yourself tells the conscious mind to look in the mirror at every opportunity and practice the smile. This self-talk process develops mind control. Your mind must first be aware, through your thought process, that you are not smiling; therefore, you must practice. As we have been told before, perfect practice makes perfect. Perfect is when the subconscious mind has learned to smile and our conscious mind now has only to conduct routine exercises to keep the subconscious telling us to smile. The technique of teaching this subconscious automatic behavior works in many other aspects of our life, as well.

There are times when it is difficult to smile, but those times are usually comforted with a smile from others. Smiles are to be desired because they are beneficial in our expressions of our faith and our hope in mankind. Smiles are to be shared as a benefit of a hope filled life.

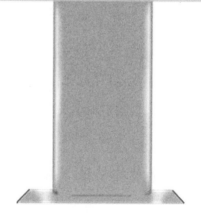

THE POWER BEHIND
US IS GREATER
THAN THE
TASK BEFORE US.

SUCCESS IS OFTEN JUST AN IDEA AWAY.

Most success stories start with just an idea; but the idea is not what makes it a success. Many ideas fail because no action is taken. All ideas require follow through with action to create any success story. Not all ideas have the potential to become successes, but if there is no follow through, one will never know.

"Follow through" is not necessarily completing the idea. For an idea to become a success, you must follow through on research of your idea, to see if the idea is plausible. You need to see if you have the capabilities (resources) to create the infrastructure for the realization of your idea. Research is the most important thing before putting a plan into action. Will I have a market for my idea, if so, who is my market and will I be able to make the idea cost affordable for those who are in my market? How will my idea be distributed? Your research must satisfactorily indicate that the idea will work. These and many other questions must be answered before you invest any mountable assets into your idea. But, you must invest something in order to see if your idea will work before you sink everything into this idea.

Ideas are a dime a dozen. In other words, they are plentiful. Johann Wolfgang bon Göethe, a German playwright, once said, "Those who carry forth their ideas are rare. Thinking is easy, acting is difficult, and to put one's thoughts into action is the most difficult thing in the world." Your idea belongs to you and will stay with you until it is developed, if not by you, by someone else.

How do we define success? "suc·cess (s...k-sµs") n. 1. The achievement of something desired, planned, or attempted: attributed their success in business to hard work." It takes many years of preparation to achieve overnight success. Preparation requires many hours of hard work. We don't want to take ideas for granted and assume they will develop without enormous effort. If an idea has merit, it deserves the energies needed to develop the idea. Work provides the source to metabolize the processes creating energies needed to sustain the idea.

Every idea is not a success; however, we should not be discouraged, and we should keep coming up with ideas, for it may be the next one that is the success. I remember when Rhonda and I made our first attempt in business. It was a total failure. We were going to open a miniature golf course. We spent several dollars on equipment, but had not prepared a business plan nor done any research. Our idea failed, and we sold the equipment many years later for pennies. In one's attempts to advance in the society of life, there will be mistakes. Those mistakes are the education needed to prevent the next mistake. Confucius might have said – "Those who 'do' make mistakes. Those who 'do not' make bigger mistake."

Successful ideas are not only those that give you financial success; successful ideas also help train, educate, heal, comfort, solve problems, and prevent crimes, playing a role that enhances lives.

The simplest and/or most complex things started with just an idea. I encourage you to pay more attention to your ideas, share them with others and take action.

THANKSGIVING IS MORE THAN TURKEY.

I look around me and see a more than comfortable home, with nice furnishings, a full cupboard; and I am definitely thankful for those things. I look outside and see trees, grass, flowers; and I am thankful for those things, as well. There are the birds, rabbits, and squirrels that I see every day, and I'm thankful for those. I see the beautiful blue sky and the sun which lightens our world every day, and I am thankful for that. I have all my limbs, you know: arms, legs, and hands. I am using my hands to type with now, and I am thankful for them. I am thankful for the cup of hot tea to my side; and that bit of dark chocolate, which a nibble every now and then, seems to make the tea a little better. I hear Rhonda taking a shower. I know it is a hot shower because she likes hot showers; I know she is thankful for that. Her feet are always cold, and I know she has the tile floor heating so it will be warm when she steps out. I know that she is thankful for that. Oh, by the way, I see the most beautiful red bird sitting on a limb just outside my window. I can't seem to stop seeing those things for which I am thankful. For these things I am thankful to God.

If we think about it, the things for which we are most thankful are traced back to God. It is through Him that all things are possible. I believe this. I see and realize this every day.

There are things that are sad in the world, but the things to be thankful for far outweigh the sadness. I believe many refuse to see these things for one reason or the other. I ask that those people just think - think of what is provided, gratis, for us to enjoy. Choose to enjoy those things that God gave us. The country in which we live "is the land of milk and honey." We just sometimes get caught up in life and fail to notice.

Enjoy your day, and stop occasionally to smell the roses. After you do, don't forget to offer a bit of thanks to God for the fragrance, beauty and enjoyment that it gives.

IT MAKES GOOD HORSE SENSE TO LEAD A STABLE LIFE.

**WARNING:
EXPOSURE TO THE SON
MAY PREVENT BURNING.**

**WALK WITH THE LORD
AND YOU WILL
NEVER BE OUT OF STEP.**

**CAN'T SLEEP?
TRY COUNTING YOUR BLESSINGS.**

**ASPIRE TO INSPIRE
BEFORE YOU EXPIRE.**

**UNDER SAME MANAGEMENT
FOR 2000 YEARS.**

**YOU ARE NOT TOO BAD TO COME IN.
YOU ARE NOT TOO GOOD TO STAY OUT.**

THE CREATION OF A FOREST
STARTS FROM A SINGLE ACORN.

This is how it happened... I was looking for my next topic and stopped on this one; when I began writing, this poem appeared. I know the source.

The Single Acorn

The wind blew and the rain came down.
To a far off land the acorn ran,
Until the soil was soft as sand and the wind ceased to blow.

All alone in a meadow dear, a small oak tree stands.
The sun brings warmth and the sky brings rain.
And the little oak tree grows.

He looks around, and not one tree in sight.
Had he been ask where to grow, he would not say nigh.
For a spot with other trees, he would have chose.

With plenty soil around his feet, his roots would bury deep.
The sun was very filling and the rain was his to keep.
Soon he grew tall and mighty, because he had no foes.

The animals from the land began to visit.
Suddenly life as an oak showed signs of hope,
For his acorns fell and the critters began to show.

Soon from out of nowhere, more trees began to grow.
He was laughing and spreading tears of joy.
The acorns he had planted are now trees tickling his toes.

Because of blessings from above and promises of old,
The tree is now a forest, of which he is the tallest.
These words are meant to show how God intends for us to grow.

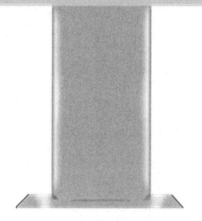

THE HAPPINESS OF YOUR LIFE DEPENDS ON THE QUALITY OF YOUR THOUGHTS.

We have somewhere between 12,000 and 50,000 thoughts in one single day (The National Science Foundation). This sounds like an enormous number of thoughts. What do we think about? We think about: an idea, a plan, an opinion, a particular person, a subject, an expectation or hope that something will happen, a feeling of respect, affection and consideration for somebody or something etc. These are just a few examples of our thoughts. Some thoughts are routine, requiring very little mental energy to perform, such as opening a door or how much mayonnaise to put on a sandwich. The thoughts that matter are life changing or character building — the ones that provide a boost to our happiness and help advance our productive lives. These thoughts have to be controlled and encouraged by our surroundings, our desires and our ambitions.

Before we go any further, I would like to make note of one of the best sources for education in this area. It is a book entitled: *What To Say When You*

Talk To Your Self by Dr. Shad Helmstetter, PhD. In his book, he spends a lot of time on thoughts. For instance, Dr. Helmstetter says we become the living results of our own thoughts and we control, in our minds, most everything in our lives. He also states that seventy-seven percent of the things we think about are negative. If you want to know how to improve your life, you must read this book.

The encouraging news is that we can change our thoughts to positive. If your mind is full of negative thoughts, these thoughts act negatively upon your body, the same way positive thoughts will act positively; you become what you think about. The confirmed theory of "Positive Mental Attitude" has been surmised by hundreds of sales trainers and motivational instructors as the most necessary thing to develop a successful "life changing" or "success achieving" life. *The Power of Positive Thinking,* written by Dr. Norman Vincent Peale, is relished by motivators as the book for changing lives through developing a positive mental attitude.

Developing a positive mental attitude is necessary to change our negative reactions to positive responses. Hope developed through faith in Christ is also another way to develop a change in our lives. Combine the two and you become stronger than you ever imagined. These two aspects of life changing peculiarities are neither drugs nor surgery. They, however, can be the most important life sustaining element to the human body.

It is absolutely necessary you have a positive mental attitude to change or control your thoughts. If you don't believe you can accomplish this task of improving or changing your thoughts, it cannot be done. Change your attitude to a positive mental attitude, controlling your thoughts with this new attitude. Drive out all negative beliefs and thoughts, then your mental and physical adaptation will begin responding positively. This will cause you to feel better about yourself, resulting in having more confidence around people. With this increase in confidence, you will notice improved experiences in your work life, spiritual life and family life. This positive mental attitude will reduce negative stress and show improvement in your physical and mental health. You will view life differently.

How does this create happiness? It makes absolutely good sense to say if you could eliminate the negative things in your life, feel better, have more friends, better financial position, better health, improved family life, and improve your spiritual life, you would be happier.

This positive thought process will anchor your beliefs (faith in God) to the "I can" instead of "I can't" thought pattern. After all, if you think you can – you're right, or if you think you can't – you're right. Mark 9:23 "...Everything is possible for him who believes."

When I was only ten years old my grandfather believed in this same philosophy when he gave me this advice: "You can do anything if you set your mind to it."

Keep your thoughts clean and focused.

THE HEAVIEST LOAD
ONE CARRIES
IS A CHIP
ON THE SHOULDER.

"Get the chip off your shoulder" is the phrase we most often hear. When this is said to you, do you know to what they are referring? Introspection will reveal why one would say such a thing to you. Something just happened that, for whatever reason, didn't go your way. You have resentment blocking your logic. But, guess what, other people notice. If you carry a chip for your entire life, it will affect you negatively and establish a negative attitude pattern. That chip will control many aspects of your life: mostly in a negative way.

A chip on your shoulder could cause you to give a bad first impression. People characterize us every day as someone they would like to know or someone they hope they never meet again. Displaying these chips will either attract those with the same chip or shun those who don't have or want a chip. Life is good and I don't want a chip to have a detrimental effect on my day. Chips can control you if you let them. They do this by controlling your thought pattern and establishing a negative outlook on life.

This chip may consist of a previous happening - a burden of some sort. It could be something that happened as far back as childhood or as recently as today. To those chips from childhood, I might simply pull a Dr. Phil and say "Get over it." These chips will hold one back, prevent a person from achieving all they are capable of achieving. We should ask ourselves why we feel this way. Then ask if it is worth the price we have paid.

This chip could be large enough to establish our whole attitude in life or small enough to ruin a good day. Either way, the sooner we get rid of it, the sooner we can make a difference in our lives. I see these chips as grudges, prejudices, disappointments, results of not getting our way, etc. Getting rid of these burdens will require change — changing our thinking. An effort will have to be made to forget and forgive. These old chips keep us looking in the past and cloud the future. These chips distort our vision of life (attitude). The fresh chips are just messing up our day.

To control these chips you will need to carry on a conversation with yourself. Ask yourself if this event in your life is important enough to sacrifice positive things that will definitely happen if you bury that chip. Sometimes we can put the quietus to problems by talking to ourselves.

We listen to ourselves without animosity. Since there is no resentment, we don't fight the answer. Sometimes we should laugh it off because our chip is so ridiculous. Chips on the shoulder are also passed down from generation to generation. Make sure you are not carrying your parents' chips on your shoulder.

We have enough to bear without these unnecessary burdens. Make a change today. Do some forgiving, forgetting, apologizing and dust off your shoulder.

Make sure that a chip is not keeping you from attending church and pursuing your salvation.

DON'T GIVE UP.
MOSES WAS ONCE A BASKET CASE.

HEAVEN.
DON'T MISS IT FOR THE WORLD.

DON'T PUT A QUESTION MARK
WHERE GOD PUTS A PERIOD.

DUSTY BIBLES LEAD TO DIRTY LIVES.

EVERY CHILD IS HOME SCHOOLED.
WHAT ARE YOU TEACHING?

EXERCISE DAILY! WALK WITH THE LORD.

FORBIDDEN FRUIT MAKES MANY JAMS.

GENEROSITY GIVES MORE HELP
THAN ADVICE.

GET RIGHT OR GET LEFT.

THE MOST IMPORTANT THINGS IN LIFE ARE NOT THINGS.

We spend so much time thinking and talking, about things (objects) such as Hummers™, ipods™, Xboxs™, Donna Karen Fashions™, Jones New York Jeans™, and plasma TVs. They have dominated our conversations and goals. I'll be the first to admit, I like these things. If we have worked hard and spent wisely, it is good to own nice things. On the other side of the coin, I don't want to catch myself envious of those who own these things, or desiring these things because others own them. You should not covet anything that belongs to your neighbor. (Exodus 20:17)

Our charge as money managers is simple. We are to work hard and spend wisely for our needs with little or no debt; for we are taught, the borrower is slave to the lender. (Proverbs 22:7) We are to give and be good stewards of God's wealth.

Some of the most important things are priceless, not because they are expensive, and not because they cost nothing, but priceless because they mean so much, - things like a meal with the family, a day at the park, or a fishing trip. There are many things that enlighten our lives as well as the lives of others: things that cause the heart to react. A simple phone call to a loved one or someone you care about, a card to remember someone on a special occasion and a visit to someone who is ill are things that show our love and enlighten lives.

There are things that give us "warm fuzzies": a pet from the pound, a Christmas parade, a play or cantata, or a baptism. There are things that we do with compassion: share a seat on the bus or allow the elderly to go before us in the grocery store checkout line.

Growing up as a sharecropper's son in a small three room house with no indoor plumbing, I can attest to the many simple things that enlightened my life: a dog that I could always call my friend, a nearby stream that provided fun in the summer, beauty in the winter and fishing in the spring and fall. There were many other similar things that country living provided. We could not afford "things," but we enjoyed what we had.

There is just as much pleasure (maybe more) in giving as receiving. Anytime we give of our time, our compassion, or simple recognition and receive thanks, we have encountered a thing that cannot be bought.

As you can see, important things are not material things but things received from life, things that have been provided for us.   The world is directing us in paths that seem to make all the material things important. Material things are good to make our lives easier, pleasant, secure, comfortable, time saving, etc. But, the things that matter are not matter at all.

Hummer is a registered trademark of General Motors Corp., 300 Renaissance Center, Detroit, MI 48265.

iPod is a registered trademark of Apple Computer, Inc., 1 Infinite Loop, Cupertino, CA 95014.

XBOX is a registered trademark of Microsoft Corp., One Microsoft Way, Redmond, WA 98052.

Donna Karen New York is a registered trademark of DK Co. which is part of the LVHM Moet Hennessy Louis Vuiton Family, 550 Seventh Avenue, New York, NY 10018.

Jones New York is a registered trademark of Jones Investment Company, Inc., 250 Rittenhouse Circle, Bristol, Pennsylvania 19007.

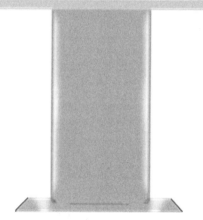

Thoughts Behind The Words

THE BEST
VITAMIN FOR A
CHRISTIAN IS
B1.

THE ONLY REAL MISTAKE IS ONE IN WHICH I LEARNED NOTHING.

We go through life with the fear of making mistakes. There are many things we fail to try because of fear. President Franklin Delano Roosevelt once said, "The only thing we have to fear is fear itself." This is a life changing lesson to learn, but it is difficult to master. Those who have mastered this art of overcoming fear have done so over a long period of time. We must remember that courage is not the absence of fear. Courage is overcoming fear with determination and this doesn't happen overnight. It is accomplished by tackling small fears, and with this sense of accomplishment, you then can progress onto larger fears. You may not completely overcome fear, but you can reduce it to a level to which you can grow your confidence. Tackling the fear of making a mistake begins with self-talk. You must ask yourself what is the worst thing that could happen. Once you realize the alternative is something you can deal with or is not detrimental to your mere existence, then you will have created less fear.

The next thing we need to work on is attitude. With a "can do" attitude, you can analyze the project in which you are fearful and reduce the amount of fear with the confidence created by having this attitude.

Also, to develop confidence you have to do some homework. Research the project and determine if it is feasible. Abraham Lincoln used a comparison process. On one side of a piece of paper, he would write down all the positive things about his idea. On the other side, he would list the negative things about his idea. He used this information to help with his decision.

You grow from your mistakes. You learn what will not work. When Thomas A. Edison was asked about failing so many times with his inventions, he replied, "I have not failed; I've just found 10,000 ways that won't work." Learning is the goal. It is very seldom that someone's first idea is the one that works. It usually has to be adjusted, regrouped, revamped, or tried in different applications. The important thing is that we must not let the "fear of trying" stop us from learning.

We make many mistakes in life. The important thing is we recognize them as mistakes and make changes to prevent the same mistake from happening in the future. We must have a good sense of recognition. This would be developed by observing outcomes from everything we attempt. In every relationship we encounter, we must observe the outcome of our actions and set goals for improving outcomes.

During my business career, I had many advertising ideas. Most did not work. There were some good residual effects, but only a few were notable. But, I did not stop advertising our business. On the contrary, I would continue to search for new and different ways to attract new customers, while continuing to use the ideas that had worked in the past.

Here is a quote that has helped me. I heard this quote from Tom Hopkins. He calls it The Champions' Creed.

"I am not judged by the number of times I fail but by the number of times I succeed. And the number of times I succeed is in direct proportion to the number of times I can fail and keep on trying."

This tells me that no success is achieved without actions and not all actions are going to be successful, but what I learn from the unsuccessful actions (mistakes) will lead me to success. If you make a mistake, you must learn from it, or you have made the greatest mistake of all.

THE PAST
CANNOT BE CHANGED ...
THE FUTURE
IS IN YOUR POWER.

Though many try, it should be obvious to us we cannot go back into the events of the past and undo them. For some reason, we tend to worry about the past. The past continues to occupy our minds, if not openly, in our subconscious. How do we, once and for all, let the past go and realize there is nothing we can change from now back to creation?

We must first realize that we cannot create a device, a time machine, or a magical potion that will take us back into the past to change the things we would want to change. However, there is something we can do that is just as powerful. We can realize our potential to create the future. Our abilities are limitless; our power and our abilities are limited only in our minds.

If we continue to depend on the abilities that the past has demonstrated, we will travel down the road we are now on and no new roads will be built.

Our "road" will become like the past and this is what we sometimes want to change.

We must have hope for the future. "Now faith is the substance of things hoped for, the evidence of things not seen" (Hebrews 11:1). We must have faith in ourselves. Our attitude should be a "can do" attitude, avoiding the "cannot do" attitude. Hope of the future is generated from the past. Jesus Christ gave us "hope" with the great sacrifice He made on the cross. Christ's death and resurrection wiped away the sins of the past and gave us "the hope" of eternal life. As a believer in Christ, confessing our sins and asking for forgiveness has the same effect today.

Our life in the past should give us hope of better things to come. If we have made mistakes in the past, we have the opportunity to learn from them and correct the future. If we have failed to do something in the past that weighs on our minds, we have the opportunity to "un-fail" (rectify) in the future. This doesn't change the past, but helps to balance the scale. If we have damaged our health in the past, it is difficult to change. But, the sooner we start, the sooner our bodies will respond. If there is something we have said in the past that we continue to regret, we have the opportunity to apologize now.

How do we make this giant step? We make one small step at a time. Just remember, if we don't like things as they exist now: (our spiritual life, our health, our work, or our family relationships), we must start changing now. If we continue to do as we are doing, we will continue to get what we are getting.

WISDOM IS THE ABILITY
TO USE KNOWLEDGE
SUCCESSFULLY.

WORRY ALWAYS GIVES A LITTLE THING
A BIG SHADOW.

WORRY ENDS
WHERE FAITH BEGINS.

WORRY IS INTEREST PAID ON TROUBLE BEFORE
IT IS DUE.

YOU SHOULD BE MORE INTERESTED
IN YOUR DIRECTION
THAN YOUR SPEED.

"YOU THINK IT'S HOT HERE?"
GOD

THE SECRET
OF SUCCESS IS
GETTING STARTED.

I have had moments when I would disagree with this statement; however, when I examine it closely, I find it is very true. I disagreed only because many times I have started something with enthusiasm only to find myself not following through and leaving the task undone to start yet another task. One of the great things about life is that we can continue educating ourselves. We can learn from our mistakes and gain knowledge, wisdom and discipline. I am learning to finish a task before beginning others. As an example, while writing these thoughts I have renewed my commitment to finish this book. We must keep motivating ourselves to complete tasks and let there be success at the end of the tunnel.

The objective mentioned in the title of this chapter is getting started. That is where the success begins. Nothing is ever accomplished without action. Action is what we are talking about when referring to "getting started." To complete a task that has never been started is impossible. Getting started is truly the secret. I have read book after book and listened to many speakers who have spoken of the secret of success. They all direct me to myself. The secret of getting started is me. Our success is all up to us and our choices, which include our attitude, work ethic, and personality. Yes, it is your choice and you can change any of these values, contributing to a more successful path. You have complete control of your success.

First, do you have the attitude for success? Do you see yourself as being successful? One thing all successful people have in common is a positive mental attitude (PMA). Zig Ziglar said it best when he said, "A positive mental attitude won't insure that you can do anything. But, it will insure that you can do anything better than a negative attitude can." With this PMA and proper preparation, you will be able to start with a goal of completion. Seeing the completed goal in your mind will encourage you to finish.

Determine your idea of success. It is hard to determine whether you are successful or not if you don't know what success is. You must not take a trip though life without a life map. You must know what your goals and ambitions are before going down the road of life. Success is different for everyone, as I would expect it to be. Many times we think of success in dollars and cents. I would label success as "achieving a desired position in life." This is the reason it will be different for each one of us. Our desired positions in life are different. Some of us want our own business. Some measure success on how well they are known in social circles. Success to some is winning a particular political office, for others it is the size of their house. Our success should encompass all aspects of life: home/family, work, spiritual, and financial. Success is only worthwhile if we succeed in all of these areas. One of my motivators is a phrase I have revered for many years. I acquired it from a series of tapes by a very popular real estate sales trainer, Tom Hopkins, "DO THE MOST PRODUCTIVE THING POSSIBLE AT EVERY GIVEN MOMENT." He has since added balance to this statement, meaning to balance all aspects of life around this statement. This has driven me to be productive in my actions and to continue asking myself if what I am doing is productive. Many times I failed to add balance to my life and centered my success strategies on business alone. No doubt it contributed greatly to my success in this area, but I missed out on the other aspects of life.

Another choice I mentioned is ethics. I believe you can maintain good ethics in business, home and community if you run all your decisions or "choices" through God first. By this, I mean see how He would handle the situation (Luke 6: 31) "Do to others as you would have them do to you." This is the secret of good ethics.

With the right attitude, a directional map, and spiritual leadership, you can achieve success, but you must get started now.

THERE IS
NO TRAFFIC JAM
ON THE EXTRA MILE.

If you are wondering why some succeed and others don't, it's because they go that extra mile. If you're in competition, you must practice more than your competitor. You must practice better. You must exert more energy. You must concentrate more. You must do whatever you do just a little bit better if you expect to win. This is going the extra mile.

Not many people are found on the extra mile. It requires the extra effort that so few are willing to exert. The extra mile is the road less traveled, but produces opportunities that do not exist on the road most traveled. Going the extra mile means you are going further than most. I admire the accomplishments of many people today, and I realize, now, that they made a choice "to go the extra mile." At some point in our lives, we need to make a choice to go the extra mile: doing something in which we would be proud and receive recognition.

My brother-in-law, Bill Britt, is a good example. His health is better than that of most people 30 years his younger. His exercise routine is very vigorous and is daily. He has been doing this for his entire life. He just had a routine physical examination and found himself in exceptionally good health. His blood pressure, his cholesterol and all the other things a physical examination checks were in excellent condition. He has gone the extra mile to maintain a high quality of physical health. If you're not in good shape physically, then you have not gone the extra mile in this area.

Don't confuse the extra mile with the last mile. The extra mile is a choice you make and not a last resort. You choose to go the extra mile if you're a dreamer. A dreamer's DREAM (determination, resources, enthusiasm, ambition, motivation) will be the vehicle needed to travel that extra mile.

I learned in order to succeed in business, you have to stand out, be better than most. The best way to do this is to do what others won't do. This is one form of going the extra mile: doing more than "what is necessary." For example, Jesus encouraged this in the Sermon on the Mount. "If someone forces you to go one mile, go with him two miles" (Mathew 5:41).

We have not given it our best shot until we have gone the extra mile. Everyone tries. Everyone wants to succeed or accomplish something outstanding. Not going the extra mile is holding them back. We are instructed to do more than others... "If you love those who love you, what reward will you get? Are not even tax collectors doing that? And if you greet only your brothers, what are you doing more than others? Do not even pagans do that? Be perfect, therefore, as your heavenly Father is perfect" (Mathew 5:46).

By not going the extra mile, we miss the smile on God's face.

THOUGHTS BEHIND THE WORDS

TODAY
IS A GIFT
FROM GOD-
USE IT WISELY.

TRY JESUS.
IF YOU DON'T LOVE HIM,
THE DEVIL WILL
TAKE YOU BACK.

Assuming that we are in mutual understanding, there is a God and there is a devil, we will pursue the topic of good and evil. God is good and the devil is evil. Christ (the Son of God) gives us hope and the devil gives us damnation. John 5:29 "And shall come forth; they that have done good, unto the resurrection of life; and they that have done evil, unto the resurrection of damnation."

The devil's temptations are abundant. Daily we encounter those temptations, and as Christians we must resist, in order to grow in Christ. Resisting is not easy; this is why they are called temptations.

The devil is always recruiting those who do not wish to fight these temptations. I believe that God puts a hedge around his followers that makes it difficult for the devil to cross. I also believe our living and succumbing to these temptations, without communication with God, will break down these hedges.

Christ welcomes us with open arms. We are secured with Him when we believe and confess his name and are buried with him in baptism. We must believe this with all our heart. We must change our lives to honor Christ as our savior and as the way to salvation. The devil does not like this. For every person Christ receives as a follower, the devil loses. The devil lost the battle in heaven, and now he is competing for your souls here on earth (Revelations 12:7).

This leaves only two choices, there is no third or fourth: there will be those on the right and those on the left (Mathew 25:33). "Choosing," to me, is not difficult. I will choose "good" over "evil" every time.

Try Jesus Christ, as you grow to know him you will grow to love him even more. It is a greater joy to know Christ but, it is your choice.

WE ARE WHAT
WE CHOOSE...
BE RESPONSIBLE.

We choose to be responsible, or we choose to be irresponsible. Once we realize this, it becomes the foundation for tomorrow. With every decision we make, we make a choice and with this choice, we direct our future. I believe that our future is directly determined by the choices we make today. If we are to change directions of our future, then we must change what we are doing today. Remember, if we keep doing what we are doing, we will keep getting what we are getting. Responsibility could be the "R" in DREAM. To complete a dream we must have: Determination, Responsibility, Enthusiasm, Ambition and Motivation. With these five success builders we can accomplish any choice we choose.

You choose whom you hang out with. This choice can be good or bad, according to the direction of the leadership. If the leadership in this association is positive, it is beneficial to good character building; however, if it is negative, it is bad character building. Many do not see the importance of choosing with whom you associate. You have the ability to choose and should choose wisely. This is one of the first steps in building your personality. We acquire many traits and indiscretions from those with whom we have close associations. If we want to be successful and responsible adults, we should not hang out with the irresponsible.

Negative thinkers always blame someone else or something else for their troubles. They seldom take blame or responsibility for their actions or lack of actions. This seems to form a comfort zone around them. Those of us who have stepped out of our comfort zone know that this might be easier, but less rewarding.

"Being responsible" is the responsible thing to do. This is the foundation of good character building and is included in *The 7 Habits of Highly Effective People* by Stephen Covey. Once we understand: life is choices we make, not something we draw from a deck of "life cards," why would we choose irresponsibility? Choose to be responsible and join the highly effective people.

WE CAN'T BECOME
WHAT WE NEED TO BE
IF WE STAY
WHAT WE ARE.

"If you keep doing what you are doing, you will keep getting what you are getting." To a very few, this might be a good thing, but to most, this means no improvement in life.

What do we need to be? Many do not recognize the potential of their minds and bodies. If, for instance, you feel you are not as smart, talented, spiritual, healthy, or courageous as others, then this message is meant for you. God wants us to be all those things.

The truth is that we are not all equal in talents, but we are talented. We can learn to be organized, and we can improve our health. We all have courage that will show when trials come. We definitely can be smarter. Knowledge comes to those who actively pursue it. God gives us the capabilities to improve all these things. We can improve our spiritually by improving what we need to be.

Many feel that we cannot be these things without sacrificing what are deemed to be virtues or traditional values. For instance, some believe that all wealthy people think that they are better than anyone else or acquired their wealth dishonestly. This can be true, but in many cases their roots could be similar to yours. In my opinion, they do not think they are better, nor are they better than others; they have just recognized the abilities God gave them and focused on their potential. According to Steven Covey in his book *The 7 Habits of Highly Effective People*, honesty and ethics were valued by all he interviewed.

I am struggling with my efforts to eliminate clutter and establish organization. I hope writing this book will help me improve in this area. I know that I am not the only one with this challenge. I have some traditional values which I now believe are false truths that have to be overcome. To be successful in eliminating clutter and improving organization, I must answer or find solutions that will convince me that my life will be improved by acting on these theories. I see people with uncluttered lives, and I am envious. Everything is so organized; their home, automobile, work seemed to be in perfect order. I often wonder what they sacrifice in order to be this way. If interviewed, someone might say, "I give it away," another might say, "I throw it away." These are answers that make sense, but what about me: I say, "I store it away." Pretty soon I run out of storage and build more storage for things I may never see again.   I have tried giving it away, and I think no one but me wants it because everyone else is oblivious to the value in this broken lamp. I can use the parts to repair other broken lamps. I am beginning to see the picture here. I am saving the broken lamp for something that will probably never happen, and I am sacrificing the peace of living without clutter, the peace I seem to admire in others. Has this cured me of my "clutteritis?" No, but I am one step closer.

As you could tell by the previous paragraph, clutter is an issue I am dealing with. Possibly you are dealing with an issue that needs to be improved. I would suggest that you take the same approach I am taking. I know that the people who live clutter-free lives have improved their lives to Gods liking. Yes, God is pleased when we improve any aspect of our lives. We are expected to be all we can be, and we can be, by utilizing all we are. We must talk to ourselves and encourage ourselves to improve our self-image. If you think you can or you think you can't ...you're right.

WE DON'T CHANGE THE MESSAGE... IT CHANGES US.

The message, as recorded in the Holy Bible, is sufficient. In recent books and movies, the message of Christ has been under scrutiny, and many believers have been upset that this would have an effect on our faith or on new believers. It is my opinion that the words written in the Bible, which have been studied now for nearly four hundred years (The Holy Bible, King James Version, 1611), are sufficient to maintain my faith and to recruit new believers.

I tend to look at the big picture, even though I know the picture is so large that I can't even begin to understand it. Keeping in this realm, I tend to trivialize those "word issues" that we dwell on and use to excommunicate our allies in faith.

I believe the big picture is: there is a God that created everything, we accept Him as our Father who displayed his love by sending his Son to earth to die on the cross, and his death and resurrection gives us hope of an eternal life with him. These accounts and instructions of how we should live our lives, to allow us to receive the promises of hope and salvation, are all written in the Holy Bible: the book we have been studying for centuries.

The messages contained in The Holy Bible are life instructions, not entertainment. They are specific and we should not change them. Even with the introduction of alleged new information, these instructions for living and for our salvation have not been changed. The degree of our faith and the care and maintenance of that faith are the issues. These issues can be fulfilled by following the messages delivered in the long standing instructions found in the Book known as The Holy Bible.

The biggest change the "message" makes is the change of direction, from lost to found: accepting the message of the cross, believing in God, Christ, and the Holy Spirit, and receiving the reward of a joyous home for our soul. Study this message and make the changes designed and written by God.

These changes, made in our heart, also contribute to other positive changes here on earth. It is noted that those, whose spiritual lives are complete with faith in God, are happier at work, healthier, more apt to succeed in business, live a better family life, help others more and, in essence, live a better life.

The message is love; it is expressly written and cannot be changed.

A CLEAN CONSCIENCE IS A SOFT PILLOW

A MAN WHO SINGS HIS OWN PRAISE...
ALWAYS GETS THE WRONG PITCH.

A SHARP TONGUE
MAY CUT YOUR OWN THROAT.

A SMILE IS THE SHORTEST DISTANCE
BETWEEN TWO PEOPLE.

A WINDOW OF OPPORTUNITY
DOES NOT OPEN ITSELF.

AN APOLOGY IS A GOOD WAY
TO HAVE THE LAST WORD.

AN OCCASIONAL LIMP IS BETTER THAN A
PERPETUAL STRUT.

ANGER IS ONE LETTER SHORT OF DANGER.

WE STUMBLE
OVER PEBBLES...
NOT MOUNTAINS.

Is it the little things that control our life? Yes, little things have an enormous effect on our daily lives. *Don't Sweat the Small Stuff...and it's All Small Stuff* is a book by Dr. Richard Carlson in which life's pebbles are observed in a pragmatic way. This book gives us simple ways to keep the little things from taking over our lives. This is a book that all should read. The earlier in life that you read it, the earlier you can see what is controlling your life. More importantly, you can learn how to take back that control.

It is not the pebbles that control our destiny. It is the way we react or respond to these little events that control our destiny. Once we learn that these pebbles are picayune when dealing with the whole picture, we can learn to "deal with them" by responding rather than reacting. I believe a large percentage of our attitude has been developed by little things that have happened throughout our lives; but, they have affected it in a negative way. If we only knew how to respond, then those little things would have a positive or no effect on our life. Just learning to handle these pebbles could change our destiny.

First, we must recognize it as a pebble. If we focus on the mountain and ignore the pebble, we will be more apt to continue our journey. The mountain is the big picture. We should not let little things block the view of the big picture. If we spend all our time and energies on the pebbles, we may lose the sight of the mountain. We may win the battle but loose the war. But, if we learn to control or reduce the small battles (accepting them as small stuff), we will be more apt to win the war. Keep focused on the mountain (the big picture).

Second, we must use the pebble to our advantage. Maybe it's not a pebble at all; maybe, it is a lesson to be learned or a warning to be heeded. We should ask ourselves: what knowledge can be gained from this pebble or what ability can be achieved by avoiding or overcoming this pebble? Am I not stronger because I have to deal with these pebbles? It will make me reach the mountain quicker and easier.

Once we recognize the pebble and learn that it is only small stuff, we can use it to our advantage by retaining the knowledge it provides, rather than stumbling. We don't want to stumble over the same pebble again or keep it on our shoulder.

Once we learn how to avoid or overcome these pebbles without stumbling, we are closer to climbing the mountain. Keep focused on the mountain (the big picture) at all times - focusing on the things that Jesus focused on. He overcame many pebbles, dealing with them one by one, so he could remain focused on the big picture. We all learn from Christ's pebbles. We learn humility, endurance, faith, hope, love, and honor and to see the mountain with our eyes closed.

It's the little things that keep us from our goals. We can always see the mountain; therefore, we don't stumble over the mountain. But, stumbling over the small pebble may keep us from reaching the mountain.

WHAT THE WORLD NEEDS IS FEWER RULES AND MORE GOOD EXAMPLES.

Here are 15 answers to "Why are there rules?" that were given on www.yahoo.com/answers. This website gives the opportunity to pose questions and then others log in and give their response to the questions. The responses are limited and then the best answer is voted on. At this writing, the voting was still in process (for the second time after a tie), and the most popular answer was not available. I stumbled on this website by accident, but I like to see what others are thinking, so I am sure I will return to check out future questions.

Why do we need rules?
- For safety reasons.
- Because there are idiots.
- Hopefully so people don't ask a lot of stupid questions.
- To prevent chaos, vandalism and other crimes.
- So you can break them.
- To protect the meek.

- You need someone to tell you what to do because of your lack of responsibility.
- So that man can keep us on a leash.
- Without rules the total world would be chaos.
- They help us to avoid decisions.
- Prevent mayhem.
- Without rules there would be anarchy.
- They are there for all humans to abide and conform to the norms of society.
- There are rules so that we can be. Without them we wouldn't exist.
- There are rules because some people are just idiots and do idiotic things.

I thought it was interesting to see the diversity in the answers. It is obvious that we have rules to keep order and prevent mayhem as one puts it. But, it is also interesting that one response tells how individual responsibility would prevent the need for rules: "You need someone to tell you what to do because of your lack of responsibility." Is this all it takes to eliminate the need for rules? Of course not, for proper rule keeping we need responsible people (good examples).

Could we exist with only responsible "good examples?" Sure we could. But, the responsible people don't understand the irresponsible people and would make more rules to control them. So we would be back with rules again. We have laws to protect ourselves: speed limits, seat belt laws, now even rules to keep us from smoking, and eating too much fat. It sometimes appears that we are a dumb society, but then who is making the rules? Someone must know that speed kills, that we are safer with a seat belt and fat makes us obese and clogs our arteries. Are these not smart people?

If only it was as easy as setting good examples and every one following, but no matter how many good examples we set, there are those who would refuse to follow. Two of the Yahoo answers referred to the fact that there are just some idiots out there.

Here in our country and other countries as well, there will always be rules. If we would all follow the example of Jesus Christ, it would make the need for fewer rules. But, Christ knew there were to be rules and he instructs us to follow them. I don't believe he would agree with rules that would encourage us to share his world with other gods. We must live by His example, and through good examples, we will draw more to him and make life here on earth more peaceful, reducing the need for rules. It is up to us to accept the rules place by God and the example has been set (Christ). It is up to us to accept the example by following the rules placed on this acceptance. Rules, which if followed, will lead to great rewards.

Call them rules or call them examples. I believe rules were put here as good examples. But, I also believe it takes good examples to follow rules.

WHEN OPPORTUNITY
KNOCKS ...
OPEN THE DOOR.

How do we know when opportunity knocks? It is a learned talent. A talent achieved by developing the proper "frame of mind" (attitude). You learn to recognize opportunity and develop the willingness to accept it. To develop this attitude, you start the way you start any day in your life— by making a choice. There is a chapter in Og Mandino's book *The Greatest Salesman in the World* that begins with this daily self-expressed quote..."I will greet this day with love in my heart." This quote, to me, expresses the proper attitude needed to recognize opportunity. If you develop this attitude and just be aware of the events happening around you, you will recognize opportunity when it knocks.

If you feel opportunity never knocks, maybe you are not doing your part. Opportunity, in its early stages, may not appear to be much at all - a choice to be made that would not be construed as an opportunity. It is according to what stage in life we are as to how big the opportunity manifests itself. This small choice may be something like reading a book, attending a meeting, furthering your education, listening to a motivational recording or hundreds of other "out of the box" self-improving activities.   We need to grow, develop, improve, challenge ourselves, never be stagnant, encourage others to grow, keep active mentally, set goals, and use time wisely. If we do these things, or even have the desire to do these things, opportunity will manifest itself.

Recognize your opportunity.   I am a big believer in "talking to yourself" and that it could make a difference between opportunity or failure. Every time you are asked to volunteer or join a group you have been given an opportunity. This is an opportunity to expand your knowledge base, your social base, learn skills such as communication, leadership, fundraising, diplomacy among other things. This creates more and more opportunities for more opportunities. When asked, talk to yourself and say "Self, if I say no what am I forfeiting, and why am I saying no? Is this an opportunity I will regret not taking?"

Make your own opportunity. You can create your own opportunity with a D R E A M. This is an acronym for determination, resources, enthusiasm, ambition and motivation. All of these qualities or attributes are necessary to create your own opportunity. Your determination is the driving force behind your dream. Without it, you will not have the willpower to complete it. <u>Resources</u> are needed to fund your dream. Resources are anything which you have and are used to produce, or in the production of, your dream. If you don't have <u>enthusiasm</u> to encourage others to help with your dream, it will be most difficult to complete. <u>Ambition</u> is the desire for success that will be needed and, without it, there will be no follow through in reaching the goal. <u>Motivation</u> is an ongoing effort to keep all the previous attributes revived and to give you the cognitive abilities to complete the dream.

Opportunities are frequent in our lives; we need only to listen and act.

WORRY IS PULLING TODAY'S CLOUD OVER TOMORROW'S SUNSHINE.

Whatever you do today affects tomorrow. The more we worry today, the more negative effects we will have on ourselves tomorrow. Worry is negative energy causing stress upon our bodies. Most worry is generated from things we have absolutely no control over. The things we worry about, statistically, have a very low chance of happening. I believe we should occupy our minds with learning, reading good books, listening to good recordings, having fun, meeting with friends and other such positive activities that would keep our minds busy. We should avoid idle time - we are most likely to worry then. Excessive worry affects our physical and mental health. To help those who are worriers, I would say, as I have said many times before, "Talk to yourself" and "Make a choice." Tell yourself: no matter how much I worry about this or that, it will have absolutely no effect on the outcome.

Why worry? Most who worry believe it is a virtue — if I don't worry about this person, it is the same as saying I don't love them. I believe love is not the issue. Worry cannot change the outcome, and it produces negative effects on our bodies. This is not the result I would expect from love. It would be better to take action on things that we can do something about rather than to worry about things we cannot do anything about. At least, this would occupy our idle time and help to prevent worry. If we are worried about the hungry, feed the hungry. If we are worried about someone who is ill, visit them and/or pray for them. Worry is not a substitution for prayer or the same as prayer. Worry should diminish with the act of prayer. Worry has the same affect on us as clutter: it does not let us function properly and clogs our minds. Clutter is stressful and has a negative effect on your life by making it difficult to find things, and it junks up your home. Worry is clutter of the mind.

I would like to share this Bible passage concerning worry: Matthew 6:25-34 "Therefore I tell you, do not worry about your life, what you will eat or drink; or about your body, what you will wear. Is not life more important than food, and the body more important than clothes? Look at the birds of the air; they do not sow or reap or store away in barns, and yet your heavenly Father feeds them. Are you not much more valuable than they? Who of you by worrying can add a single hour to his life? "And why do you worry about clothes? See how the lilies of the field grow. They do not labor or spin. Yet I tell you that not even Solomon in all his splendor was dressed like one of these. If that is how God clothes the grass of the field, which is here today and tomorrow is thrown into the fire, will he not much more clothe you, O you of little faith? So do not worry, saying, 'What shall we eat?' or 'What shall we drink?' or 'What shall we wear?' For the pagans run after all these things, and your heavenly Father knows that you need them. But seek first his kingdom and his righteousness, and all these things will be given to you as well. Therefore do not worry about tomorrow, for tomorrow will worry about itself. Each day has enough trouble of its own."

Don't worry, be happy and healthy.

I HOPE YOU DIDN'T MISS THESE GREAT LINES.

"But, if you limit yourself by not realizing all things are possible, then you have, in essence, cheated yourself."

"Character is built by one response at a time or destroyed by one reaction at a time."

"There is nothing more gratifying than to take an old worry and eliminate it."

"Lying not only deceives others, but deceives our self-image as well."

"Work with what you have today, and make plans for tomorrow, but don't use tomorrow's resources to live on today."

"Anger takes over the brain and the results are never beneficial to the decision making faculty."

"It takes several peoples' ideas to form a single opinion that is appropriate for a majority."

"The "purpose" is a vision of fulfillment; a vision that is channeled through spiritual and intellectual filters, utilizing your talents, with the "purpose" fueling your efforts."

I HOPE YOU DIDN'T MISS THESE GREAT LINES.

"The act of kneeling, without a believing faith, will give you nothing more than sore knees."

"The controls are within me, but the know-how is within God."

"I have learned one thing in communicating: there is no one thing."

"We must keep focused, overcoming these moments, and building our "faith-esteem.""

"But the things that matter are not matter at all."

"Hope of the future is generated from the past."

"By not going the extra mile, we miss the smile on God's face."

"We should avoid idol time – we are most likely to worry then."

"Worry is clutter of the mind."

"Again, I am not speaking of the "Big Ones," but many burdens are camouflaged opportunities."

"Neighbor is more relationship oriented than geographical oriented."

"This desertion or spiritual laziness can lead to faith deterioration."

SUGGESTED READING

What to Say When You Talk to Yourself by Dr. Shad
Helmstetter.
Powerful New Techniques to Program Your Potential for
Success!
April 1987, ISBN 0-671-63519-0 (paperback)

Thinking for a Change by John C. Maxwell
11 Ways Highly Successful People Approach Life and Work
April 2003, ISBN 0-446-52957-5

Lead Like Jesus by Ken Blanchard and Phil Hodges
Lessons from the Greatest Leadership Role Model of All
Time.
2005, ISBN 0-8499-0040-9 (hardcover)

Better Than Good by Zig Ziglar
Creating a Life You Can't Wait to Live
2006, ISBN 9-781-59145-400-7

Attitude is Everything by Keith Harrell
10 Life-Changing Steps to Turning Attitude into Action.
Revised Edition 2005, ISBN 0-06-077972-1 (paperback)

As A Man Thinketh by James Allen
1992, ISBN 0-88029-785-9 (hardcover)

The Power of Positive Thinking by Dr. Norman Vincent Peal
The Greatest Inspirational Bestseller of Our Time
First Fawcett Crest Edition: Apirl 1963
First Ballantine Books Edition: June 1982
First Columbine Trade Paper Edition: August 1996
ISBN 0-449-91147-0

Who Moved My Cheese by Spencer Johnson, M.D.
An A-Mazing Way to Deal with Change in Your Work and in
Your Life.
1998, ISBN 0-399-14446-3 (hardcover)

I highly recommend all these books. After you read these,
you may contact me by email and I will supply a list of
additional readings (robert@thoughtsbehindthewords.com).

ABOUT THE AUTHOR

Robert makes his home in Murfreesboro, Tennessee with his wife Rhonda. His beginnings were in the extreme rural farm area known as Yellow Creek. In this very humble environment, living in a small three room house on his grandfather's farm, he first began his search for fulfilling  a dream. This dream required his leaving the farm to pursue other areas of interest, overcoming challenging circumstances.

Throughout life, he has experienced contact with consumers of products, beginning with selling corn and watermelons from the farm and helping his uncle at a community grocery. This sense of service gave him something the farm did not. He pursued this interest and began his retail experience at the lowest level (sweeping the floor) leading to a ten year management career with a regional retailer, leaving only to establish his own business.

In 1981, Robert and Rhonda, opened a retail jewelry operation and within four years had developed the business into a total of seven individual stores. He remained in the jewelry business for twenty-three years and retired in 2004 after selling the business. Robert discovered his writing career after deciding to interpret the sayings on church marquees, which resulted in this book. He intends to continue writing: his new passion and something that only words can express.

Photograph by LifeTouch Portraits, Galion, OH

For more information and to order this book go to
www.thoughtsbehindthewords.com